ENDORSEMENTS

Very few people have more zeal and interest in the Christian supernatural than Sid. I have known him for many years, and I appreciate what his programming has done to open people up to the supernatural. I know this book will be used in a similar way.

Dr. Randy Clark
Overseer of the Apostolic Network of Global Awakening
Founder of Global Awakening

When I got this manuscript for Sid's new book I knew it would be good, but it exceeded all of my expectations for its scope, its depth, and the fresh, powerful insights into God's ways that it contains. There are many good books being written, and a few great ones, but every now and then there is a transcendent book that everyone should read. This is a transcendent book everyone who seeks to know God should read.

RICK JOYNER
Founder, MorningStar Ministries
Best-selling author of *The Final Quest*

I have known Sid Roth since 1984, and he has never wavered from his calling and burden: to see God's supernatural power at work and to see our Jewish people saved. Sid is the most fearless, unashamed soul-winner I know and today, well into his seventies, he is more on fire for the Lord than the day I met him. Here, he lays out his life message, encouraging every believer to step into God's supernatural life and power.

DR. MICHAEL L. BROWN
President of FIRE School of Ministry
Host of nationally syndicated talk radio show, *The Line of Fire*
Author of *The Real Kosher Jesus, Our Hands Are Stained with Blood,*
and *Whatever Happened to the Power of God?*

Sid Roth is an amazing man of God, a pioneer of the end-time Messianic revival, and a leader who has touched countless lives, opening them up to seek the power and reality of the living God. He has become an authority throughout the world on the supernatural realm of God's moving. His enthusiasm for the things of God is contagious, and his zeal is irresistible. I have known Sid for decades and I can bear witness of him as a man of integrity and zeal. He is as passionate and on fire for God now as he was then—even more so. His life is in itself a witness and a testimony to the supernatural power of God.

JONATHAN CAHN
New York Times best-selling author of
The Harbinger and *Mystery of the Shemitah*

If your spirit is thirsty this is a must-read book. My friend, Sid Roth, will take you by the hand and guide you on a journey through the Gospel's supernatural realm. You will be positioned to grow, mature, and step into the role you were created to fulfill in such a time as this.

JOHN BEVERE
Author/Minister
Messenger International

IT'S SUPERNATURAL!

DESTINY IMAGE BOOKS BY SID ROTH

They Thought for Themselves

Sooner Than You Think

Heaven Is Beyond Your Wildest Expectations
(with Lonnie Lane)

Supernatural Healing
(with Linda Josef)

Truth Seekers
(with Mike Shreve)

Supernatural Experiences

There Must Be Something More!

The Incomplete Church

IT'S SUPERNATURAL!

WELCOME TO MY WORLD, WHERE IT'S
NATURALLY SUPERNATURAL

SID ROTH

IT'S SUPERNATURAL! PRESS
It's Supernatural! and Messianic Vision, Inc.
4301 Westinghouse Blvd.
Charlotte, NC 28273

Cover design by Eileen Rockwell
Interior design by Terry Clifton

ISBN 13 TP: 978-0-7684-1086-0
ISBN 13 eBook: 978-0-7684-1087-7
ISBN 13 HC: 978-0-7684-1465-3
ISBN 13 LP: 978-0-7684-1464-6

For Worldwide Distribution, Printed in the U.S.A.
1 2 3 4 5 6 7 8 / 21 20 19 18 17

CONTENTS

FOREWORD

By Tony Kemp

Sid Roth and his television program *It's Supernatural!* have been used by God to literally change my life and ministry. In the spring of 1972, when I was 16 years old, I received Jesus as my Lord and Savior at a very traditional Baptist church. At that time there was a move of God among young people in my community. One young man received a vision of Jesus that radically transformed his life. I saw the change, witnessed how full of Jesus he had become, and watched as he received the ability to speak in a supernatural language by the power of the Holy Spirit. Later, through the laying on of hands by an Assembly of God minister, I too received the baptism in the Holy Spirit, spoke in tongues, and soon after was called into ministry.

I spent five years serving as a youth pastor, 20 years as an associate pastor, and then became a senior pastor. During those 26 years I saw maybe 100 people receive Jesus as Savior and Lord and perhaps ten people healed of minor physical problems. Believe me, I was extremely frustrated at the lack of results I was seeing in ministry!

I had graduated from college, been to Bible school, and studied theology, but I was not getting biblical results. My frustration ignited a hunger for a move of God. I knew there was more, but I didn't know how to receive "the more of God" I was thirsting for.

One day I came across the television program *It's Supernatural!* I listened to Sid and his guests talk about how God was working supernaturally today. These ordinary people were describing how they witnessed and experienced God performing signs, wonders, and miracles in their lives. I found myself watching one program after another. I would watch *It's Supernatural!* six to eight hours a day and sometimes more.

As I watched and listened to Sid and his guests, I saw a supernatural pattern emerge. An intense spiritual hunger led to a revelation of the Word and, when followed by obedience, always produced a manifestation of the miraculous! This spiritual hunger was accompanied by persistence, perseverance, a patient faith, and an attitude that said, "I will not quit seeking God until I receive what I am believing for! I *will* receive a fresh revelation and visitation from God and *I will never be the same!*"

Another truth I discovered from the guests and Sid as they shared their testimonies of the presence and the power of God was that whenever the Father wants to do a miracle, He always gives you an instruction. When you obey, miracles and answers to prayer follow.

When I put into practice the principles of the Word that I learned on *It's Supernatural!*, the blind saw, the deaf heard, wheelchairs were emptied, the crippled walked, and diseases like diabetes and cancer were healed. Growths and tumors disappeared instantly, and body parts appeared where there were none! People received dental miracles, experienced supernatural weight loss, and had metal in their bodies replaced with new bone! Even physicians were amazed at the miracles! People were saved in restaurants, malls, churches, and communities. Many were delivered from demons, freed from bondage, and filled with the Holy Spirit!

By definition, God is a supernatural being and He wants to do supernatural things through ordinary believers in His Son, Jesus. As I have shared how my life and ministry were impacted by the revelation of the Word I was exposed to on *It's Supernatural!*, others have begun to watch the program and have had miracles occur in their lives and ministries.

You see, revelation is the jurisdiction of your faith. Where you do not have a revelation, you cannot have faith. Where you have the revelation of the Word, you find your faith. When and where you find your faith you experience the person and the presence of God and you encounter the anointing and power of the Lord Jesus!

Sid Roth is a man who knows firsthand by experience the revelation and reality of Jesus the Messiah.

Sid's new book will be the catalyst for you to discover the ways and wisdom of the Father so you too can manifest the works of Jesus! As you read this book, you will learn that any believer can work wonders through intimacy with the Messiah. Get ready as Sid takes you on a journey with Jesus so you can show people the true nature of the Gospel and say, *"It's Supernatural!"*

INTRODUCTION

I became a believer in the Messiah in 1971 at the height of the Charismatic Renewal. As there were very few Jewish believers at that time, I became an instant celebrity. A major newspaper in Washington, D.C. published my testimony on the front page. Then Kathryn Kuhlman read the article and invited me to appear on her national television show. Even before I had read through the Bible, I was sharing my testimony all over the United States.

For those who are not familiar with Miss Kuhlman, she had the greatest miracle ministry I have ever witnessed! After doing two television shows with her, going to her meetings, and meeting her privately, she made me an offer. She said, "I wish you lived in Pittsburgh. I would love to mentor you." But I turned her down. At that time, I thought she was just a "normal" believer. After all, when I read the Gospels I saw that Jesus' followers operated in the miraculous. I thought all believers would be like her. I didn't realize she was one of a kind. It is one of my biggest regrets!

I am one of the few survivors of all this acclaim and notoriety. I was never discipled or mentored or went to Bible school. It is only by God's grace that I did not fall. But because of my path, it took me many more years than necessary to understand the invisible world.

Many wonder why I emphasize miracles. It is not for the sake of the miracle. It's to demonstrate the reality of God to a world that is speeding on a one-way road to hell! I have found that the strongest Jew, Muslim, New Ager, and even atheist is arrested by the demonstration of a miracle. Then it is easy to present the Gospel and lead them to Jesus! Do you think Peter would have led 3,000 Jewish people to Jesus without signs and wonders?

For example, I received a great testimony from one of our TV viewers named AJ. This woman was an atheist who became a New Ager. She was searching online for videos about angels and came upon our program. AJ had never even read the Bible, but she said a prayer with me and got saved. And it did not stop there. She became addicted to watching our TV show, *It's Supernatural!* (Note: Our 24/7 high-definition *It's Supernatural! Network* is available on every smart phone and computer in the world through our free app. Find it in the app store by searching for my name, Sid Roth.) All this ministry happened to this one woman by watching our program. Then AJ said she felt something leave her body. God sovereignly delivered her of New Age demons. But it gets better! Her whole family got saved and was water baptized together at their new church!

My heart's desire is to speed up your growth in the Spirit. After over 40 years of interviewing God's best men and women who operate in the supernatural, I am uniquely qualified to mentor you.

We are about to have a heavenly invasion. We are about to see the greatest awakening in history. We are about to see the greatest miracles in history. We are about to see the greatest number of people saved in history.

If I could have chosen to be born in any generation, it would be this generation. The first Jewish believers in Jesus walked in amazing miracle power. In the Catholic Church you need three miracles to become a saint. But the least follower of Jesus in the first Church could demonstrate three miracles in *one day!* This miracle power over the centuries was watered down to the point that any Christian who walked in miracles was so unique they could get their own television show! It's about to change. And you are chosen to be a saint! By the way, the New Testament says we are all saints. The word *saint* is short for "sanctified one." Any born again believer is sanctified in Jesus.

Years ago, I heard a message from a leading teacher who worked for Oral Roberts. One day he was assisting Oral in a healing line. Then, suddenly, God opened his eyes to the invisible world. He had x-ray vision. He could see the brains of the people waiting in line. They were very big. Then he could see their spirits. They were tiny, almost anemic. We have a generation that has spent more time developing our minds than our spirits. Our spirit man is starving for food and drink. I want to be your personal trainer for your spirit. I wish I had these revelations from over 40 years of investigative reporting when I first became a believer!

Strap on your seat belt. It's an incredible time of multiplication, advancement, growth, and miraculous harvest. First things first, though. In order for me to mentor you in the supernatural, you need to know the times and seasons.

IT'S SUPERNATURAL!

Discover why it's so vital for you to know that this is your season of sand and stars!

Chapter 1

YOUR SEASON OF THE SAND AND STARS

Then the Angel of the Lord called to Abraham a second time out of heaven, and said: "By Myself I have sworn, says the Lord, because you have done this thing, and have not withheld your son, your only son—blessing I will bless you, and multiplying I will multiply your descendants as the stars of the heaven and as the sand which is on the seashore; and your descendants shall possess the gate of their enemies. In your seed all the nations of the earth shall be blessed, because you have obeyed My voice."

—Genesis 22:15–18

This is your season of sand and stars! I believe this statement is a prophetic declaration over your life. It's time for you to claim what belongs to you through promise and inheritance.

So many followers of Messiah Jesus are living beneath their privileges. For some, they live ignorant of the promises of God and never appropriate them in their lives. For others, they have received poor or misguided teaching about the availability of God's promises.

Perhaps one of the most dangerous lies has been that God does not move miraculously anymore—that the "day" of the supernatural came to a close after the canon of Scripture was compiled. This is not a secondary issue or a small matter, as some would think. What you do with the supernatural power that God has made available will determine how much of your destiny you walk in on earth. You have an assignment to fulfill that, I believe, demands supernatural assistance.

While this is not a "heaven or hell" issue, the fact is that many people who are on their way to hell are waiting to see a demonstration of God's supernatural power in *your life* and mine.

This is our highest motive for *It's Supernatural!* It accomplishes two very important goals: 1) Mentors believers on how to operate in the supernatural benefits and tools that Jesus made available, and 2) reaches out to those who do not yet know Jesus as Messiah but are intrigued by the supernatural.

Scripture tells us that within the heart of every human being is an ache—a longing for a taste of eternity (see Eccles. 3:11). Could it be that when someone experiences the supernatural, inborn desire for eternity is awakened all the more? I know this is true!

The Jewish people have a spiritual DNA that will result in world salvation!

So, how will this all unfold? In order for you to start walking in the supernatural power of God, experience miraculous results, and make the world around you hungry to know Jesus, you must understand and appropriate the promise of God that was originally made to Abraham, the great patriarch of the faith.

Understanding Your Promise

In Genesis 22, God makes this outstanding promise to Abraham—a promise that directly impacts your life today!

> *I will certainly bless you. I will multiply your descendants beyond number, like the **stars** in the sky and the **sand** on the seashore. Your descendants will conquer the cities of their enemies. And through your descendants all the nations of the earth will be blessed—all because you have obeyed me* (Genesis 22:17-18 NLT).

Today, it is evident that God has used Abraham's physical seed, the Jewish people, to bless all mankind. The Jewish people have been responsible for a disproportionate number of inventions, scientific discoveries, and Nobel Prizes. More importantly, our Messiah came through the seed of a Jew. Paul says in John 4:22, *"salvation is of the Jews."* The Jewish people have a spiritual DNA that will result in world salvation! If we are to step into a season of increased supernatural demonstration where miracles become normal, we must understand the importance of this promise.

A New Species of Being

However, most cannot imagine how the descendants of Abraham will ever be as numerous as the sand on the seashore or as the stars in the sky. What they don't understand is that God was painting a picture of His New Humanity (translated "One New Man" in most Bibles, but in the Greek it means "one new humanity"). Paul calls this New Humanity made up of Jews and Gentiles a new species of being that never previously existed. In Second Corinthians 5:17, Paul says, *"Therefore, if anyone is in* [the Messiah] *he is a new creation* [Greek: new species of humanity]; *old things have passed away; behold, all things have become new."*

Paul explains the One New Humanity in Ephesians 2:15-16 (NIV): "[Messiah Jesus'] *purpose was to create in himself one new humanity out of the two* [Jew and Gentile], *thus making peace, and in one body to reconcile both of them to God through the cross."*

Is this One New Humanity Jewish or Gentile? Paul gives the answer in Galatians 6:15: *"For in* [Messiah] *Jesus neither circumcision nor uncircumcision avails anything, but a new creation."* Also in Galatians 3:28-29 Paul explains, *"There is neither Jew nor Greek, there is neither slave nor free, there is neither male nor female; for you are all one in* [Messiah] *Jesus. And if you are* [Messiah's] *then you are Abraham's seed, and heirs according to the promise."*

Do We Stop Being Jewish or Gentile?

Does this mean that we stop being a Jew or a Gentile when we become part of the Body of Messiah? No. In the natural there are males and females and there are Jews and Gentiles. Paul is obviously speaking of another dimension—the spiritual. As we yield to the spiritual, we make room for our One New Man as part of the spiritual seed of Abraham. This is what Paul meant in Galatians 3:29: *"And if you are* [Messiah's] *then you are Abraham's seed, and heirs according to the promise."* This is how the season of the sand and stars will fulfill Abraham's vision. God has a specific call for Jews and Gentiles in the natural, just as He has a specific call for male and female. Although there is no Jew or Gentile, male or female in the Spirit, we should never spiritualize the natural. If we do, we will miss God!

God reveals more about this subject of stars in the Old Testament. In Daniel 12:3, God tells us how to be wise in this life: *"Those who are wise shall shine like the brightness of the firmament, and those who turn many to righteousness like the stars forever and ever."*

 Get ready for your catalyst from heaven.

This book has an anointing and supernatural wisdom to make you one of God's stars! It will equip you to not be a spectator but to enter into the season of the sand and stars. It is the season of the greater signs and wonders and the great harvest. The curtain is going up. Your name is being called. John 14:12 says, *"He who believes in Me, the works that I do he will do also; and greater works than these he will do."* I want to take this opportunity to mentor you to walk in the same and even the greater miracles that Jesus promised!

What is this new species of humanity that never previously existed? Let me introduce you to the One New Humanity, the Body of Messiah, Jesus. God started with physical Jews to form His Body. Next, He introduced Gentiles to be part of His Body. Just before His return at the *"fullness of the Gentiles,"* He will once again show mercy to the Jewish people. Romans 11:25 says, *"For I do not desire, brethren, that you should be ignorant of this mystery, lest you should be wise in your own opinion, that blindness in part has happened to Israel until the fullness of the Gentiles has come in."*

The Body of Messiah is incomplete until two events take place. First, there must be a great Jewish harvest. This has already begun because we are in the season of the sand and the stars. Then this Jewish harvest will be the catalyst for the greatest miracles and Gentile harvest in history. According to *Webster's Dictionary*, the word *catalyst* means "a substance that causes a chemical reaction to happen more quickly." Get ready for your catalyst from heaven.

Right here is the key to participating in the greatest outpouring of miracles, signs, and wonders that the world has ever known. I can personally testify that we are living in this season of sand and stars, as I am watching Jewish people come to the Messiah in unprecedented numbers. This is not exclusively relevant to Jewish people or the Messianic movement; this information is relevant to you because it gives you a clear revelation of the incredible season in which you are living.

I believe we are about to enter the season of the greater works. We will not only demonstrate the miracles Jesus did, but the creative miracles are coming!

Recognize Your Season

The "sons of Issachar" in the Old Testament are examples on how to respond to the season we are in.

> *From the tribe of Issachar, there were 200 leaders of the tribe with their relatives. All these men understood the signs of the times and knew the best course for Israel to take* (1 Chronicles 12:32 NLT).

These leaders recognized first and responded second. When you recognize the season in which you are living, it gives you clarity on how to respond effectively. The sons of Issachar recognized the times they were living in and thus were able to instruct Israel on the best course of action to take.

I often wonder if the people of God living right now are fully aware of the season they are currently in. Although "greater works" are prophesied to come in the future, I do believe how much we see of the "greater" is determined by what we do with the "same works." We will see more when we start recognizing the urgency of the hour we are living in and respond accordingly.

I believe we are about to enter the season of the greater works. We will not only demonstrate the miracles Jesus did, but the creative miracles are coming!

In order to fulfill this great assignment, however, it's very important that you recognize who you are in Messiah Jesus. To access the incredible promises of "sand and stars," supernatural outpouring, miraculous demonstration, and supernatural exploits, there is a position you need to stand in. You need to live life *from heaven to earth.* In other words, you need to be naturally supernatural!

So Heavenly Minded We *Are* Earthly Good

We who believe in Jesus live in two worlds. Jesus lives in us on earth and we live in Jesus in heaven. This is an awe-inspiring fact— one that our mortal minds have a difficult time wrapping around. Even though it is beyond our understanding, it is not beyond our grasp. Colossians 1:27 says, *"Messiah in you, the hope of glory."* And Paul says God has *"raised us up together, and made us sit together in the heavenly places in Messiah Jesus"* (Eph. 2:6).

Even though you are living in a mortal body on planet Earth, right now you are also seated with Jesus in the heavenly places, spiritually speaking. You have been positioned *in the Messiah,* not by your efforts or works but because of His work on the cross. This is why the apostle Paul reminds us:

If then you were raised with the [Messiah], *seek those things which are above, where* [Messiah] *is, sitting at the right hand of God. Set your mind on things above, not on things on the earth* (Colossians 3:1-2).

He is saying that because you have been raised with Messiah Jesus and are seated with Him in the heavenly places, this needs to be the lens through which you see life. This is your supernatural vantage point. In order to walk in God's promises, you need to first be able to see them as real and relevant for your life today. In the pages ahead, I want to equip you with some tools that will help you see from a supernatural vantage point. When you pray from heaven, begin to see satan under *your* feet.

Too many believers in the Messiah are, unfortunately, too earthly minded to be of any heavenly good. We are not seeing as many miracles and supernatural demonstrations of power that we *could*, not because of an unwillingness from God's end but an unwillingness from our end. To live "naturally supernatural," the first thing we must do is change the way we think and the way we see. It's time for followers of Messiah Jesus to, once again, think *from* heaven.

How You Can Participate in History's Great End-Time Revival!

Understanding your position in Messiah Jesus is absolutely essential if you are going to be a part of welcoming this prophetic season of sand and stars. In order for you to think from heaven's perspective, you must remember that even though you are living in the world, you are not *of* the world (see John 17:16). Jesus did not use this language, "of the world," to make people detach from bringing His Kingdom to society. To *not* be "of the world" is to reject the world's system of thinking and behavior. As a follower of Jesus, you are called to follow *His* example of behavior, thinking, and living. Remember, you are a new creation in the Messiah. Earlier in this chapter, I reminded you that you are a completely new species of being. That is how powerful the blood of Jesus is to change your identity! In view of this truth, you need to think of yourself as a person seated in heavenly places but an ambassador on earth.

Let's look one more time at Galatians 3:28-29:

> *There is neither Jew nor Gentile, there is neither slave nor free, there is neither male nor female; for you are all **one** in* [Messiah] *Jesus. And if you are* [Messiah's], *then you are Abraham's seed, and heirs according to the promise.*

Paul is speaking of the two worlds in which we live—the natural and the supernatural. Although I function as a Jewish man in my earth suit, I am always aware I am seated in the control center of heaven in Jesus! And simultaneously, Jesus lives inside of me on earth! I am so heavenly minded I *am* earthly good. I have a role to play in the natural realm as a male and a Jew. If I changed any of this, I would not fulfill my destiny.

In the same way, God wants to use *you*. You live in both the natural and the supernatural realms at the same time. You may function as a Jewish or Gentile person in your "earth suit," but when it comes to your spiritual position you are seated in the control center of heaven. Let that truth settle into your thinking. How would your life change today if you lived mindful of this reality? I can promise you this—your prayers would begin to change. Your faith would start to increase. Your willingness to take risks, step out, and operate in the power of God would skyrocket.

Earlier, I wrote about the importance of recognizing the season you have been placed in. *This is the season of sand and stars.* This is the time of the greatest harvest in history. This is a catalyst moment in history where ancient prophecy is unfolding and the people of God are being mobilized to welcome the greatest revival and outpouring of the Spirit ever! And yet, it's shocking that we can go through our entire lives either blind to the urgency of this season or, even worse, aware of the season's invitation but blinded to our position in Jesus.

When you combine recognizing the season with understanding your identity in Messiah Jesus, you will be positioned to operate in God's supernatural power in a level you've never experienced before. The problem is that the supernatural has stopped being natural for followers of the Messiah. It's time for that to change. It must if you are going to fully embrace God's end-time assignment!

When it comes to your spiritual position you are seated in the control center of heaven.

Your Revelation of Identity Determines Your Fulfillment of Destiny

In the natural realm, the Jew has a specific role and the Gentile has a specific role in the end times. This is why Paul placed such emphasis on the One New Humanity. The One New Humanity is the Body of Messiah, the new creation, the new species of being. This is why it is so important for you to recognize your position, appropriate the promises, and demonstrate God's power. If you don't know who you are in Jesus, you will never believe you are qualified to fulfill the destiny He has for you.

Although I am Jewish and a male, in the spirit I am a new creation foremost. Paul explained in Galatians 2:20, "*I have been crucified with* [the Messiah] *it is no longer I who live, but* [the Messiah] *lives in me.*" The real me, my spirit, lives in a temporary male, Jewish "earth suit," but my emphasis must be the heavenly, new-creation man. My natural man must decrease and Jesus must increase to the point of totally controlling my life.

Do you understand what this all means for you—*a new creation* in Messiah? Jesus controlling your life is not a limitation or restraint; it is surrendering to ultimate freedom. If Jesus were a tyrant with hostile motivations, then yes, yielding control to Him would be a problem. That's not Jesus. More than any human being alive, Jesus the Messiah desires what is best for you. He is championing you to fulfill your destiny. He has made provision for you to walk in every grace and gift of the Holy Spirit so that you can walk in the fullness of His power on the earth.

The truths contained in this book will remain mere concepts unless you firmly grasp that in the Messiah you are a new creation. I don't want to give you concepts that increase your head knowledge; I want to help activate you to fulfill the call of God in your life. The tools I provide in upcoming chapters will change your destiny. Whether you are a businessperson, pastor, doctor, lawyer, or educator. Whether you are a stay-at-home mom, banker, athlete, or movie actor. No matter what you have been called to *do*, you have been given a new-creation identity.

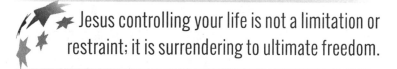

Jesus controlling your life is not a limitation or restraint; it is surrendering to ultimate freedom.

I want to equip you to play your role in embracing God's great harvest season. This is a pivotal moment that history has been moving toward. Remember God's promise to Abraham in Genesis 22:17?

Blessing I will bless you, and multiplying I will multiply your descendants as the stars of the heaven and as the sand which is on the seashore; and your descendants shall possess the gate of their enemies.

Note how many times God assures Abraham of His commitment to this promise:

- *"I will bless you."*

- *"I will multiply your descendants."*

- *"Your descendants shall possess the gate of their enemies."*

When God says "I will," He means it. It's a promise, and Scripture tells us that God cannot go back on His promises (see Num. 23:19). It's impossible for God to lie, and this promise includes the One New Humanity, so that means you! The time is now. *Are you ready?*

Part One

YOUR SUPERNATURAL POSITION AND POWER

You have been sovereignly destined by God to live in this unique moment in history. You are no accident, and your salvation is not happenstance. You were delivered out of the bondage of sin, on a pathway to eternal separation from God, for such a time, for such a season, and for such a purpose. This sounds exciting, but there's a problem...a big one. Too many followers of Messiah Jesus don't know what or Who they have living within them.

God has authorized you to walk in His supernatural power. This is not just available to an exclusive, elite group; this blessing has been reserved for every believer in Jesus. In order to move in supernatural power, you first need to recognize your supernatural position and power—this is the *authority of the believer*.

In Part One, you are going to receive a revelation of the authority you have in Messiah Jesus. Once you understand this supernatural position and power, you will be able to operate the supernatural tools that God has entrusted to you.

Chapter 2

YOUR GOD FACTOR

But God, who is rich in mercy, because of His great love with which He loved us, even when we were dead in trespasses, made us alive together with [Messiah] (by grace you have been saved), and raised us up together, and made us sit together in the heavenly places in [Messiah] Jesus.

—Ephesians 2:4-6

Your identity in Jesus has an enemy. The devil is on a mission to keep you living ignorant of who you are and what you have inherited through Messiah Jesus. He knows that the moment you have a full revelation of your covenant rights, you will never desire to live beneath it. The mere thought of a lifestyle of compromise will be appalling to you, not because you are concerned about whether or not God "still likes you" or whether you have gotten "too close" to the line of sin. These become non-issues for the believer who is awakened to his or her position in the Messiah. When you know who you are and how God sees you, that is the standard you will want to live according to. The problem is that many believers are in a state of identity crisis.

In Hosea 4:6, God states that *"My people are destroyed for lack of knowledge."* Notice which people are destroyed for the lack of knowledge—*My people*. God's people! Even more than sin and temptation, lack of knowledge is perhaps the greatest weapon aimed against followers of Messiah. Satan does not want people to step into their *God factor.*

Your God factor is simply this—walking in 24/7 awareness and experience of the presence of God inside of you. He walks with you. When you walk, He walks too. When you move, He moves. When you step out in bold faith, He is there to back you up. Believers need to become more in tune with the fact that Messiah Jesus in them is the hope of glory (see Col. 1:27). The world around you needs hope, and they are given glimpses of hope when they see the glory of God released through you. This happens when you start living naturally supernatural.

To keep you from fulfilling your destiny, the enemy has formed weapons against you. Even though Scripture promises that *"No weapon formed against you shall prosper"* (Isa. 54:17), you need to make sure that you don't embrace satan's lies as truth. Be on guard. The devil knows that if he cannot overcome you, he can sneak in with crafty half-truths that, if believed, will shut down the God factor from operating in your life. Remember, he wants to keep you ignorant to the truth that God Himself lives inside of you.

Here are some weapons the enemy uses to keep you blinded to your God factor.

The Weapon of the "Half-Grace" Message

One of the most popular deceptions being embraced by followers of Jesus today is the false promise of the false grace message (also known as *hyper* grace). This lie has shipwrecked the faith of many believers and has prevented them from fulfilling their destiny in God. This is how destructive believing this lie is.

Many years ago, well-respected author and minister Dr. Derek Prince gave a talk about legalism and grace. His ministry recently published his talk in book form. Dr. Prince, who is in heaven now, was considered one of the world's finest Greek scholars and Bible teachers. So when the book came out, I really wanted to know his insight on this subject. At the time he gave this talk, legalism was at its height. The emphasis in the Church was on what *not* to do, such as smoking, dancing, wearing certain clothes or makeup, and watching worldly movies. But this legalism put Christians under great bondage. There was little joy and freedom. Derek repented and said he wished he hadn't emphasized sin so much and emphasized grace.

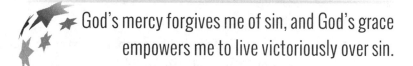 God's mercy forgives me of sin, and God's grace empowers me to live victoriously over sin.

But now the pendulum has swung to the other extreme where grace is overemphasized. When the popular grace message first started, many who were raised under legalism gravitated toward this teaching. Many young people also embraced it. I call it the half-grace message. Why? Because holiness is left out. Many times it's not what the half-grace message says but what it doesn't say! It seems we humans get stuck in one ditch or the other. The first ditch of legalism will cost you your joy and probably decrease your effectiveness as a witness to the unsaved. The other ditch, half-grace, is even worse. It could cost you your destiny in God and even your salvation!

The Weapon of Distorted Holiness

Holiness is not religion's idea. It is God's idea. God says in Hebrews 12:14, *"Pursue...holiness, without which no one will see the Lord."* I want to see the Lord in this life and throughout all of eternity. God says in Romans 2:4, *"the goodness of God leads you to repentance."*

There is a whole generation of Christians that does not understand grace, sin, repentance, and holiness. Let's define grace. Grace is God's enabling power to overcome sin. This is why it's so important to recognize the difference between the mercy of God and grace of God. God's mercy forgives me of sin, and God's grace empowers me to live victoriously over sin. Because of God's mercy, I am the righteousness of God in Messiah Jesus (see 2 Cor. 5:21); because of God's grace, I am empowered to live righteously. Mercy positioned me as righteous in Messiah, and grace equips me to walk out this new identity! Both mercy and grace are aimed at sin—a topic that is often skirted around and sometimes completely ignored in the Christian world today.

Sin is the reason Jesus died. It is what separates you from God (see Isa. 59:2). Sin is violating God's Word and its consequences are severe. In fact, they are deadly. Examples of sin are sex outside of marriage, marriage not between a man and woman, child sacrifice (abortion), addictions of all kinds, gossip, lying, slander, and New Age practices. The job of the Holy Spirit is to convict us of sin. We should celebrate this conviction because it always leads us to victory and equips us to live in holiness. If the enemy can keep the people of God from living holy lives, he will keep them from walking out their destiny and sustaining the supernatural in their lives.

The Weapon of "One-Time Repentance"

The topic of conviction is also under attack these days. Remember, the Holy Spirit convicts you because He has your best interests in mind. He wants to help you live victoriously over sin. He wants to protect you from bondage and torment. He wants to lead you along the path of life, and sin always leads to death. Spiritual death. Death of relationships. Death of dreams. Death of destiny. Death of health. Death of freedom. Even physical death. Sin is deadly; Holy Spirit conviction is life-giving!

When conviction happens, we have two choices. We can harden our hearts and ignore His nudge or we can repent. Repentance is telling God you are sorry in Jesus' Name and the power to change your behavior through grace.

Some *mistakenly* believe you repent once at salvation and *never* have to repent again. They are dead wrong. John addressed *believers* and corrected this error in First John 1:8-9:

> If we say that we have no sin, we deceive ourselves, and the truth is **not** in us. **If** we confess our sins, He is faithful and just to forgive us our sins and to cleanse us from all unrighteousness.

Also, Paul settles it in Hebrews 10:26-27:

> If we sin willfully after we have received the knowledge of the truth, there no longer remains a sacrifice for sins, but a certain fearful expectation of judgment.

Many churches, television preachers, and Christian musicians don't talk about sin, repentance, judgment, and holiness. Hollywood, television, the education system, and peer pressure mock biblical righteousness. But God says in First Corinthians 6:9-10:

> *Don't you realize that those who do wrong will not inherit the Kingdom of God? Don't fool yourselves. Those who indulge in sexual sin, or who worship idols, or commit adultery, or are male prostitutes, or practice homosexuality, or are thieves, or greedy people, or drunkards, or are abusive, or cheat people—none of these will inherit the Kingdom of God* (NLT).

This issue is life critical! In the last book of the Bible, God says, "*Outside the city* [New Jerusalem] *are the dogs—the sorcerers* [drug addicts], *the sexually immoral, the murderers* [including abortion], *the idol worshipers, and all who love to live a lie*" (Rev. 22:15 NLT). Do you want to live in the City of God? Then live a repentant life. Instantly repent the moment you realize you have sinned.

Prayer of Salvation

Perhaps you are reading this and you have *never* repented of your sins. I want to encourage you to pray this prayer to be born from above. If you are a believer in Jesus, say this prayer for forgiveness for your unrepented sins.

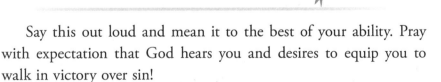

Do you want to live in the City of God?
Then live a repentant life.

Say this out loud and mean it to the best of your ability. Pray with expectation that God hears you and desires to equip you to walk in victory over sin!

> *Dear God, I am a sinner. Against You and You alone have I sinned, for which I am so sorry. Please forgive me*

for the following specific sins in Jesus' Name. (Now state the specific sins including the sin of unforgiveness. The Holy Spirit will show you exactly what you need to repent for. You do not have to dig anything up. The blanket prayer takes care of what is not specifically brought to remembrance.) According to Your Word, You remember my sins no more. Now that I am clean, I ask Jesus to come inside of me and be my Lord. Amen.

The Weapon of "Compromised Christianity"

The world is plunging rapidly to the Sodom and Gomorrah level. But what is worse is the Church is also compromising. Some are saying God's morality changes as society changes. Wrong! God says in Malachi 3:6, *"For I am the Lord, I do not change."* The New Covenant says the same thing in Hebrews 13:8: *"Jesus* [the Messiah] *is the same yesterday, today, and forever."* What this generation is missing is a clear understanding of the *fear of God.*

I did a study on the *healthy* fear of the Lord and wanted to share it with you. I am not fearful of God. But I am fearful of hurting Him and losing His presence. He is too good, too loving, and too compassionate for me to be separated from Him. King David's prayer in Psalm 51:11 expresses this same longing: *"Do not cast me away from Your presence, and do not take Your Holy Spirit from me."*

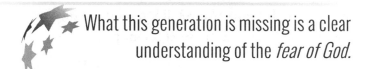 What this generation is missing is a clear understanding of the *fear of God.*

Five Benefits of a Healthy Fear of the Lord

When I did my study about the fear of God, here are five amazing benefits I discovered:

God Will Hear You

[He] *was heard because of His godly fear* (Hebrews 5:7).

God Will Heal You

Don't be impressed with your own wisdom. Instead, fear the Lord and turn away from evil. Then you will have healing for your body and strength for your bones (Proverbs 3:7-8 NLT).

You Will Be Satisfied and Not Visited by Evil

The fear of the Lord leads to life, and he who has it will abide in satisfaction; he will not be visited with evil (Proverbs 19:23).

Your Children Will Be Protected

In the fear of the Lord there is strong confidence, and His children will have a place of refuge (Proverbs 14:26).

You Will Have Riches, Honor, and Life

By humility and the fear of the Lord are riches and honor and life (Proverbs 22:4).

Remember, a healthy fear of the Lord will protect you from sin, safeguard your life from compromise, and most of all keep you in tune with the supernatural reality of the Spirit of God living inside of you. The fear of God ensures that you live mindful of the God factor because it helps you to live aware of His constant presence with and in you.

It Gets Even Better in Heaven!

Just think of it—when you go to heaven, it gets much better! I have interviewed many who have died from a medical viewpoint, went to heaven, and been told it was not their time to die. So they were sent back to earth. One of my friends died and when in heaven he was told about me and that we would become friends. He was also a Jewish believer in Jesus. His recollection of what he saw in heaven was very detailed. I especially liked what he had to say about two rooms in heaven. The first was the library. It had books about us. It recorded all we did and all we were supposed to do. The amazing thing is that for believers in Messiah Jesus, it only had the good things we did. What was bad was totally erased!

The other room I liked was the "parts room." It was a warehouse of body parts. Angels were waiting for prayers to bring them to earth. If you need a new kidney, heart, liver, or leg, it's waiting there for you. There is no sickness in heaven; only wholeness. Nothing is out of order in heaven. Solutions are waiting in heaven for God's people to bring to earth. There are blessings reserved in heaven that are waiting for your prayers—your access. Angels are waiting to be sent on assignment, responding to you speaking the Word of God. While you don't command angels, you do have the ability to declare God's Word, which dispatches these angelic beings on supernatural assignments! These are the benefits of walking in your God factor.

God wants to release resources from heaven into the earth. He accomplishes this, primarily, through people who have the power of heaven living within them through the Holy Spirit. The question is, *do you know what is yours to access?*

God wants to release resources from heaven into the earth. Do you know what is yours to access?

Just like my friend told me about the spare body parts in heaven, I believe there are answers and solutions in heaven that are just waiting for God's people on earth to pull them down through prayer.

In order to pray this way, you need to know every promise in God's Word is *yours!* And it's yours now!

Do You Want to Know God's Will and Purpose for Your Life?

I want to conclude this chapter by talking about one of the most frequently asked questions among Christians and unbelievers alike: "What is God's will and purpose for *my* life?"

People are often frustrated because they think they are not getting answers to this question. I think they are asking the wrong question. With great confidence, I can say that that I *know* God's will for your life: "*Your Kingdom come…on earth as it is in heaven*" (Matt. 6:10). The will of God for your life begins with you asking one key question: *God, what are You doing in the earth right now and how can I participate?*

God filled you with Himself   the Holy Spirit—so that through your willing and obedient life He could advance His Kingdom in this world. Think about it! You are filled with the power and the presence of the Kingdom of God. This is what Paul was writing about in Romans 14:17, when he explained that "*the kingdom of God is not eating and drinking, but righteousness and peace and joy in the Holy Spirit.*" Pay attention to the connection—*the Kingdom of God is in the Holy Spirit.*

There is a day when the Messiah is literally, visibly, and physically returning to the earth. At this point in time, the Kingdom of God will come fully. In the meantime, every believer in Jesus is commissioned to go into all the world and preach the Gospel of the Kingdom. This Gospel is both a message and demonstration of power. One chapter later, in Romans 15, Paul describes how the Gospel is fully preached:

For I will not dare to speak of any of those things which [Messiah] has not accomplished through me, in word and deed, to make the Gentiles obedient—in mighty signs and wonders, by the power of the Spirit of God, so that from Jerusalem and round about to Illyricum I have fully preached the gospel of [Messiah] (Romans 15:18-19).

Notice that the Gospel being fully preached is directly linked to *"mighty signs and wonders by the power of the Spirit of God."*

I want to help you fully preach the Gospel. It's more than simply sharing a message of words. God wants His people to preach the Gospel with words and demonstrate it with power. In order to do this, you need to live mindful of the God factor—God's Spirit living inside of you. You need to stay on guard against demonic distractions that war against you fully expressing your God Factor. Finally, you need to understand that your purpose on earth is to release the presence of the Kingdom of God—the Holy Spirit—in whatever sphere of influence God has placed you. Don't wait until tomorrow!

Chapter 3

YOUR POWER SEAT OF PRAYER AND AUTHORITY

Behold, I give you the authority to trample on serpents and scorpions, and over all the power of the enemy, and nothing shall by any means hurt you.

—Luke 10:19

This can't be happening to me! For months I had a demon pummel me—blow after blow. I prayed, confessed Scripture, and nothing seemed to work. I know this was allowed in my life for your benefit. I believe my experiences will give you the greatest revelation you have ever received concerning your place of authority in Messiah Jesus.

From Victims to Victors

Most believers know nothing of the invisible world. It's like before the microscope was invented we would have laughed if someone said there were millions of living organisms swimming in a glass of water. But it was true whether we could see it or not. Our microscope to the invisible world is the Bible. Not only does the Bible teach us about the millions of demons flying around that are invisible to the naked eye, but God's Word shows us how to have victory over them!

The problem is that as long as you remain unaware of your authority, you will not use it. Basic sense, right? You will not activate what you don't know you have. This revelation of spiritual authority over the enemy is something that Jesus Himself considered basic. The "only" authority the enemy has is because of believers' ignorance of these basic teachings.

You read in Luke 10 where the 70 disciples returned to Jesus, sharing testimonies of their miraculous works. They reported to Jesus with a sense of awe and joy, *"Lord, even the demons are subject to us in Your name"* (Luke 10:17). Jesus responded in an unusual way:

> *I saw Satan fall like lightning from heaven. Behold, I give you the authority to trample on serpents and scorpions, and over all the power of the enemy, and nothing shall by any means hurt you. Nevertheless do not rejoice in this, that the spirits are subject to you, but rather rejoice because your names are written in heaven* (Luke 10:18–20).

It was almost as if Jesus was saying, "You shouldn't be really impressed by this. You should assume that diseases and demons are subject to the authority of My name. What should really fill you with joy is the fact that your names are written in heaven!" I'll break it down even further. Jesus was saying that walking in authority over the enemy should be normal.

The problem? The ones who should be walking in victory are falling like victims. This is because too many believers do not understand their *power seat* in Jesus. In the previous chapter, we studied the position of the believer—one who is seated in the Messiah in the heavenly places. This position is what gives you access to the authority in Jesus.

Our microscope to the invisible world is the Bible.

Your Authority Over the Devil

The devil is a kleptomaniac. Why do I say that? The Bible says in John 10:10, *"The thief does not come except to steal, and to kill, and to destroy."* The Greek word for "steal" is *klepto*, so the devil is a stealing maniac! The Mayo Clinic's definition of kleptomania is "the recurrent failure to resist urges to steal items.... Kleptomania is a serious mental health disorder."[1] God has given me insight into how the crazy devil has stolen health, wealth, and family from us. It's high time we took back what has been stolen from us by this thief. In fact, one step better is positioning yourself to *not allow* the thief to steal from you at all. To protect yourself from his attacks, you need to walk confident of the authority Jesus has given you over the devil.

The books of Galatians, Ephesians, Philippians, and Colossians give us understanding into the unseen realm. You should spend a great deal of time in these books. Ephesians explains how to access the greatest power and authority in the universe. The devil knows once you access this authority he can't have his way with your family, your health, your finances, and your destiny. Paul says God *has already* blessed you *"with every spiritual blessing in the heavenly places"* (Eph. 1:3). Where is this blessing located? In heavenly places. How do we access heaven while still in our earth suit?

First, we pray for the spirit of wisdom as Paul shows us in Ephesians 1:16–22. I encourage you to pray this prayer from Ephesians every day out loud and personalize it. (Also, Ephesians 3:14–20 should be personalized and prayed out loud often.)

Ephesians 1:16–22 reveals that Jesus is seated at the right hand of God the Father in heaven:

> *[I] do not cease to give thanks for you, making mention of you in my prayers: that the God of our Lord Jesus the [Messiah] the Father of glory, may give to you the spirit of wisdom and revelation in the knowledge of Him, the eyes of your understanding being enlightened; that you may know what is the hope of His calling, what are the riches of the glory of His inheritance in the saints, and what is the exceeding greatness of His power toward us who believe, according to the working of His mighty power which He worked in [Messiah] when He raised Him from the dead and seated Him at His right hand in the heavenly places, far above all principality and power and might and dominion, and every name that is named, not only in this age but also in that which is to come. And He put all things under His feet, and gave Him to be head over all things to the church.*

He was seated *after* God demonstrated His mighty power by raising Him from the dead! Imagine the power of God that raised Jesus from the dead! That *same* power is available now to you. Jesus is seated in His power seat above *every* name! What are some of these names? Cancer, heart trouble, diabetes, high blood pressure, and poverty are a few examples. God placed *all* these names under the feet of Jesus.

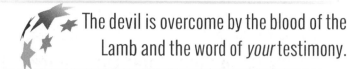

The devil is overcome by the blood of the Lamb and the word of *your* testimony.

Paid in Full

God also made us alive when He raised Jesus from the dead. He seated us in the same *power seat* as Jesus. A seated position at the right hand of God positionally means His victory and our victory is assured. In the Greek when Jesus said, "It is finished" on the cross, it meant our sins, sicknesses, and debt were *paid in full!* Then God *raised us* up and seated us in Jesus in heaven.

> *But God, who is rich in mercy, because of His great love with which He loved us, even when we were dead in trespasses, made us alive together with* [Messiah] *(by grace you have been saved), and raised us up together, and made us sit together in the heavenly places in* [Messiah] *Jesus* (Ephesians 2:4-6).

I want you to get this picture—you are seated in Jesus at the right hand of God. Because you are in His Body, *all names* are under *your* feet. When you pray every day, picture yourself in your *power seat,* seated in Jesus in heaven. Now use your two greatest weapons—the blood and the Name of Jesus—from your power seat.

The devil is overcome by the blood of the Lamb and the word of *your* testimony (see Rev. 12:11). The foreshadow of this was Passover in the Old Testament. The death angel could not harm the Jewish people if they applied the blood of a lamb on their doorpost. If the shadow had so much power, imagine what the blood of *the* Passover Lamb—Jesus—can do! How do you apply it to your situation? Today it is applied by speaking it out loud. This is how you were saved (see Rom. 10:9-10). Remember, the Greek word for "saved" also means delivered and healed!

How to Be Invincible: Experience the Supernatural Benefits of Jesus' Blood

The secret to exercising the authority that comes from your power seat in the Messiah is the blood of Jesus. You need to know what benefits it provides and how to activate the blood in your life. I am going to share some of the supernatural benefits of Jesus' blood, and then I will share about how I personally applied His blood in my life when dealing with the devil. Anything I can do, you can do better!

The Blood Provides Remission of Sin

> *Without shedding of blood there is no remission* (Hebrews 9:22).

This one benefit would have been enough. Jesus' blood is so powerful that it makes complete remission for every sin I have ever committed and washes me totally clean. Remission means obliterating the sins as if they had never been committed. But there is so much more!

The Blood Releases Conquering Power

> *And they have overcome (conquered) him* [the devil] *by means of the blood of the Lamb and by the utterance of their testimony* (Revelation 12:11 AMPC).

The blood of Jesus makes you invincible against the devil. You were never meant to be a victim of the enemy; you were destined to be victorious!

The Blood Contains the Life of God

For the life [breath] of the flesh is in the blood, and I have given it to you upon the altar to make atonement for your souls; for it is the blood that makes atonement for the soul (Leviticus 17:11).

The blood of Jesus is alive! His blood is more than even the largest demon can handle. There is no more powerful substance in the universe! The very life of God flows in the blood of Jesus. This same life that brings healing, wholeness, deliverance, and blessing actually flows *in you.*

*Then Jesus said to them, "Most assuredly, I say to you, unless you eat the flesh of the Son of Man and drink His blood, you have no life **in** you"* (John 6:53).

Every time you take communion, be sure to reaffirm the river of the supernatural life of Jesus' blood flowing in you! And wherever in your body you need healing, the river flows. *"Everything will live wherever the river goes"* (Ezek. 47:9).

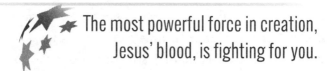 The most powerful force in creation, Jesus' blood, is fighting for you.

The Devil Cannot Cross the Blood Line

For the Lord will pass through to strike the Egyptians; and when He sees the blood on the lintel and on the two doorposts, the Lord will pass over the door and not allow the destroyer to come into your houses to strike you (Exodus 12:23).

You have an enemy and his weapons are aimed at you. Yet the Bible promises that no weapon that the devil tries to use against you will succeed. It cannot cross the blood line!

> *But no weapon that is formed against you shall prosper* (Isaiah 54:17 AMPC).

> *The blood of sprinkling that speaks better things than that of Abel* (Hebrews 12:24).

The same blood that translated you out of darkness and brought you into the Kingdom of God has the power to transform your entire household.

The blood is speaking on your behalf. Think about it. The most powerful force in creation, Jesus' blood, is fighting for you. Your job is to agree with what it says. Through faith and obedience, stand strong against the strategies of the devil. He will come to test you. Look at Isaiah 59:19 (remember, the scribes put in the punctuation, not God). This is how it reads with proper punctuation: *"When the enemy comes in, like a flood the Spirit of the Lord will lift up a standard against him"*! The devil trembles every time you say the Name of Jesus and apply the blood. Remember, the puny demon is being swept away by a flood of the power of the blood! Your response: The blood will not just speak for you automatically—you need to declare the decree of the Lord. When the enemy comes against you, you need to do what the apostle Paul instructs:

> *Therefore take up the whole armor of God, that you may be able to withstand in the evil day, and having done all, to stand. Stand therefore* (Ephesians 6:13-14).

Stand firmly in the power and authority of Jesus' blood and make yourself invincible against the devil!

The Blood and Your Household

The two spies told Rahab the harlot they could not guarantee protection for her and her family when Israel conquered Jericho:

> *Unless, when we come into the land, you bind this line of scarlet cord in the window through which you let us down, and unless you bring your father, your mother, your brothers, and all your father's household to your own home* (Joshua 2:18).

God's perfect will is that *none* should perish but that all people should come to eternal life through Jesus the Messiah (see 2 Pet. 3:9). God wants to save your entire household!

In the Old Testament, the language points to blood shed on behalf of a household. With Rahab the prostitute, God makes provision to save her and her household through the binding of a "scarlet cord." This could be viewed as a shadow for the blood of Jesus that would be spilled in the New Covenant.

Earlier, when the Passover was being established, every man was instructed to *"take for himself a lamb, according to the house of his father, a lamb for a household"* (Exod. 12:3). One lamb slain per household. Again, this is a prophetic foreshadow of what the blood of Jesus would make available to *whosoever* would believe in His redemptive work on the cross. The heart of God is for families, households, and entire lineages of people to be transformed by the power of Jesus' blood.

Consider Acts 16 as one example of how these Old Testament shadows find their substance in the New Testament. God supernaturally delivers Paul and Silas from their prison shackles, along with loosing all of the other prisoners from their chains. The jailer is terrified, knowing that the penalty for all of these prisoners breaking free would be his life. As he gets ready to kill himself, Paul and Silas stop him, assure him that all of the prisoners are still there, and proceed to preach the Gospel to him. The jailer specifically asks what *he* must do to be saved. Paul and Silas reply, *"Believe on the Lord Jesus* [the Messiah], *and you will be saved, you and your household"* (Acts 16:31). We are used to talking about how Jesus' blood was shed for *"me"* on an individual and personal level, but this same blood is so powerful that it has the ability to transform entire families! Households! Generations! Believe that the same blood that translated you out of darkness and brought you into the Kingdom of God has the power to transform your entire household.

Apply the Blood

Plead the blood of Jesus. I don't hear people use this language too often anymore, but it is more relevant—and needed—now than ever. Create a bloodline over your house, over your family, over your business, over your mind. Ensure that every part of your life is covered in the blood of Jesus. What does this look like? Jesus' blood made complete provision for you to be spotless before God. The Bible says that because of Jesus' redemptive work, you are the righteousness of God *in Messiah Jesus* (see 2 Cor. 5:21). Don't let the devil remind you of past repented sin. It doesn't exist! That is why God calls you righteous! Every area of your life should have the resurrection power of God flooding in and through it.

Plead the blood of Jesus over everything. Do it in the morning, and do it again at night. Over your children. Over your finances. Over your health. Over your future. This is not some magic formula or religious mantra. By *pleading* the blood of Jesus, you are making a declaration before heaven, earth, and even the powers of hell that *this area of life is under the authority of Messiah Jesus.* The devil cannot cross the bloodline because he cannot steal what is *not* his to take. The devil will try to make you think the blood is not working. Your reaction: give him more blood! *"Through faith and patience inherit the promises"* (Heb. 6:12). You *win* if you do not give up!

God, the Perfect One, has reconciled you to Himself through the redemptive work of Messiah Jesus.

The Blood Bought You Access into God's Glory

In the Old Covenant, the glory of God was unapproachable. None could enter into the manifest presence of God apart from following strict protocol. Yet there are times we catch glimpses of communities of people—namely, the priests—experiencing that weighty glory of the Lord manifesting in physical form. Consider this example:

> *Also King Solomon, and all the congregation of Israel who were assembled with him before the ark, were sacrificing sheep and oxen that could not be counted or numbered for multitude. ...indeed it came to pass, when the trumpeters and singers were as one...that the house, the house of the Lord, was filled with a cloud, so that the priests could not continue ministering because of the cloud; for the glory of the Lord filled the house of God* (2 Chronicles 5:6,13-14).

An animal sacrifice was required in order for the glory of God to *fill* the house. In this case, the specific "house" was Solomon's temple. In the Old Covenant, the glory filled a structure created by man; in the New Covenant, the glory fills a structure created by God Himself. That temple is your body!

Remember, God's ultimate goal was never to fill something made by the hands of man with His glory. Jesus' blood accomplished what no animal sacrifice could ever do—it brought sinful man into a realm that only the sinless could enter...and live (see Heb. 10:4). God has flooded your entire body with His glory. You have so much glory it will leak on everyone you meet.

Don't let any lying demon rob you of this peace.

> *And through him God reconciled everything to himself. He made **peace** with everything in heaven and on earth by means of* [Messiah] *Jesus' blood on the cross. This includes you who were once far away from God. You were his enemies, separated from him by your evil thoughts and actions. Yet now he has reconciled you to himself through the death of* [Messiah] *Jesus in his physical body. As a result, he has brought you into his own presence, and you are holy and blameless as you stand before him without a single fault* (Colossians 1:20-22 NLT).

Meditate on that profound truth: God, the Perfect One, has reconciled you to Himself through the redemptive work of Messiah Jesus. This reconciliation involves your complete forgiveness of sins, yes, but also it means that you have been *brought into his own presence.* What brought you there? The blood that *"made peace with everything in heaven and on earth"* (Col. 1:20 NLT).

This is fact: the blood of Jesus brought you into the glory of God and, even further, has brought the glory of God into *you.* It doesn't matter what you feel, what the devil is whispering to you, or what you have done. Even if you have sinned and fallen short of God's glory, simply repent from your heart and remember what the Bible says about your standing before God: *"but now in Messiah Jesus you who once were far off have been brought near by the blood of*

Messiah" (Eph. 2:13). This is truly your *power seat* of authority in the Messiah, and no one can take this from you!

You are the temple now, according to the apostle Paul:

> *Or do you not know that your body is the temple of the Holy Spirit who is in you, whom you have from God, and you are not your own?* (1 Corinthians 6:19)

Your temple is filled with God's glory because the Holy Spirit lives in you! The devil has no access to this place of authority and privilege—only you. Use it. Plead the blood of Jesus—yes, for protection, but also for access into the holiest place of God's presence: "*having boldness to enter the Holiest by the blood of Jesus*" (Heb. 10:19).

Remember and Announce the Power of Jesus' Blood by Taking Communion

The early believers placed a great emphasis on taking communion. We should never make this become commonplace or ritualistic. Every time you partake of communion, you are reminding yourself of your inheritance and authority in the Messiah—you've inherited "*great and precious promises*" (2 Pet. 1:4), and you've been authorized to walk in victory over the powers of darkness.

> The blood of Jesus and the believer's authority are not mere theological concepts. They can mean the difference between life or death, victory or defeat in our lives.

When you consider the historic context of the New Testament, the early followers of Jesus had wine instead of water with their meals. Thus, this gave them the ability to consider the power of Jesus' blood every time they ate!

They didn't take communion once a year or once a month or even once a day. They had communion three times a day with every meal. Every time you take communion, believe you are a little more healed until it fully manifests.

My Journey of Overcoming Demonic Torment

The blood of Jesus and the believer's authority are not mere theological concepts. They can mean the difference between life or death, victory or defeat in our lives, depending on what we do with them.

This first became revelation to me when I was personally buffeted by a demon of satan. Paul had the same problem as we read in Second Corinthians 12:7-9:

> *And lest I should be exalted above measure by the abundance of the revelations, a thorn in the flesh was given to me, a messenger of Satan to buffet me, lest I be exalted above measure. Concerning this thing I pleaded with the Lord three times that it might depart from me. And He said to me, "My grace is sufficient for you."*

In order for us to overcome demonic torment, we need to understand how the spiritual world operates. This is why I like to talk with those who operate in revelatory gifts—prophets and seers. I have interviewed many seers over the years and they have given me amazing revelation. Much of what you read in this section of the chapter came through my friend Dr. Keith Ellis, one of the most accurate seer/prophets I know. A seer can see into the invisible world with unusual clarity. They see demons and angels. I was praying with Keith about my problem with this demon. It was preventing me from going to sleep, and once I did fall asleep it kept waking me up. This caused much fear, which made things worse. The problem was not insomnia but a demon.

During the day I started to suffer from brain fog. While praying with Keith, he saw a band around my head in the spirit. The demon put it there to confuse my thoughts. Keith would pray, and he would see it leave and the band would disintegrate. Any believer can do the same whether you see it or not. Then the brain fog would lift!

In another instance, I had a pain in my knee. I had just exercised and probably strained it, I thought. But Keith saw a band around my knee, similar to what he saw around my head. When he prayed for the band to be removed, the pain left. I have found demons are like skunks. Even after the skunk leaves, there is an odor. The demon is also like a spider and can leave a web or band or residue. You don't have to be a seer to remove this spider web. Just keep the pressure on by speaking out loud, "I hold the blood of Jesus against you. You must leave and go to the feet of Jesus. You are under my feet!" You put the pressure on the demon by being persistent, enforcing the victory you have in Jesus. You speak to the demon or the residue and it must leave. Also, speak to your body and command it to be healed.

I am personally convinced there is a spirit of infirmity behind *every* sickness. And there is demonic activity behind every family problem or relationship problem. Some are the result of generational curses. Some are the result of demonically induced fear. For instance, when you go to the doctor the first question is, "What sicknesses run in your family?" I am so glad Jesus became a curse so we do not have to bear the penalty of the curse! (See Galatians 3:10,13.) The problem is so many people accept what the Bible clearly tells them to reject. We accept sickness, torment, and oppression, either thinking that God is using it to teach us a lesson or we simply don't know how to come against it victoriously. Either way, it's time we stop accepting what God wants us to reject. We need to have an *attitude* when it comes to dealing with the demonic realm!

Returning to my story, when I prayed with Keith, he could see the demon. Then he would pray in the name of Jesus, and just as the Bible says in James 4:7, *"Resist the devil and he will flee* (Greek: as in terror) *from you,"* the demon would leave. But a few minutes later it would return. It was then that I realized its strategy. Initially, I thought my prayers did not work. I thought the demon never left. But Keith could see what was happening in the invisible world. Sure enough it left at the commanded declaration of the name of Jesus. However, it circled around and came back. It was trying to make me think my prayers were of no effect.

The powers of darkness are trying to convince you that your prayers are not working. What happens if they succeed? You stop praying. You cease being persistent in prayer when you accept the lie that your prayers are not accomplishing anything. This couldn't be further from the truth.

Demons are afraid of a believer who knows his or her authority in the blood and Name of Jesus.

The Blood with an Attitude

This spirit of infirmity kept coming back to afflict me, trying to make me feel like my prayers were not working. Then I prayed one time like this: "The blood of Jesus come on you!" I prayed it with an attitude and in a very loud voice. Keith saw the demon leave instantly. I realized how much power is in the blood, just like Revelation 12:11 says, *"And they overcame him by the blood of the Lamb and by the word of their testimony, and they did not love their lives to the death."* I boldly gave testimony to the most powerful force in all the universe, the blood of Jesus. The Scripture promises that I overcome the devil through the *blood* and the *testimony* (speaking the "blood" out loud).

The next time I prayed more boldly, even in a commanding voice. This time Keith saw this gnat (that's what I called it) shake its head from side to side as in fear. It left. Now, even though I couldn't see the gnat, I imagined it shaking its head as if it is saying, "He got me again," and leaving in fear. Here is the truth. These demons are afraid of a believer who knows his or her authority in the blood and Name of Jesus. How long will they attack you? How long do you have to pray? Until they know you will never give up.

This applies to sickness, emotional problems, family problems, and financial problems. As long as you resist and keep up the pressure, you will win. The demonic world takes advantage of our ignorance and fear. God says in Hosea 4:6, *"My people are destroyed for lack of knowledge."*

This insight explains why many who are healed see the same symptoms return a day later or even months later. When that happens, they conclude that they weren't healed! But the truth is they were healed the minute that spirit of infirmity left. It just circled around and returned. That was when they should have gotten an attitude of indignation and yelled, "Go in the Name of Jesus the Messiah of Nazareth. The blood of Jesus is on you! I hold that blood on you whenever you come near me!" You are saying, "Enough is enough, devil!" You are saying, "I will hold my ground! I will keep standing, declaring, and believing!" Evil spirits are seeking a resting place, so it's quite common for them to leave a person and then come back again.

This is what Jesus referred to in Luke 11:24–26. When an unclean spirit leaves its "home" (a person), it *"goes through dry places, seeking rest.*" Finding no rest, the demon decides to return back to its "home" in the person and finds it empty, swept and put in order. After the original fight against the demon, the person has stopped reading and meditating on the Bible, praying in tongues, and worshiping and thanking God. Not only does the demon find a place of rest in the person, but it brings seven more evil demons. And now the pain, sickness, or depression is worse. Now that you know the truth, you can win *every time.*

It's Time to Torment the Devil

When the enemy comes against you, remind him—on the basis of God's Word—what's in store for his future.

> *Then He* [Jesus] *will also say...*"*Depart from Me, you cursed, into the everlasting fire prepared for the devil and his angels* [demons]*"* (Matthew 25:41).

> *The devil, who deceived them, was cast into the lake of fire and brimstone where the beast and the false prophet are. And they will be tormented day and night forever and ever* (Revelation 20:10).

One of the highest mysteries I have learned is to keep the pressure on the demon that is coming against me. As I spend a great time praying in tongues, my discernment has increased. I can feel the demons. But often they hide from me in a cloud of residue or stay further away so I can't feel them. So when I see their evidences like sickness, fear, worry, insomnia, etc., I speak by faith *often* during the day: "The blood of Jesus is upon you! I command you to go to the feet of Jesus!" That's what I mean by keeping the pressure on.

Here's an additional strategy for defeating a demonic attack: Every time I feel or see evidence of the demonic at work, that is my reminder to worship God. I thank God for His Name that I can use. I thank God for His Son's powerful blood. I thank God for His love. I thank Him for His forgiveness and for His healing. I thank God my name is written in the Lamb's Book of Life. The demon will quickly get the hint. Every time he attacks, I praise and worship God more! I sing out loud in tongues. I am not focusing on the demon's attack; rather, I am magnifying God.

One more thing I learned. My words attract demons or angels, the Holy Spirit or evil spirits. The more negative I am, the more I attract the evil spirits. The more I speak in tongues, praise God, quote Scripture, and speak only things that edify, the more the presence of God surrounds me. We are called to speak Good News. Let the nonbelievers have the job of criticizing and talking negative!

 My words attract demons or angels, the Holy Spirit or evil spirits.

Scriptures to Use Your Authority

*I am able to do exceedingly abundantly above all that I ask or think, according to the power that works **in** me* (see Ephesians 3:20).

*May blessing (praise, laudation, and eulogy) be to the God and Father of my Lord Jesus (the Messiah) Who **has** blessed me in Messiah with **every** spiritual...blessing in the heavenly realm!* (Ephesians 1:3 AMPC.)

[For I always pray to] the God of my Lord Jesus the Messiah, the Father of glory, that You may grant to me a spirit of wisdom and revelation [of insight into mysteries and secrets] in the [deep and intimate] knowledge of You. By having the eyes of my heart flooded with light, so

that I can know and understand the hope to which You have called me, and how rich is Your glorious inheritance (in me)...and [so that I can know and understand] what is the immeasurable and unlimited and surpassing greatness of Your power in and for me who believes, as demonstrated in the working of Your mighty strength, which You exerted in Messiah when You raised Jesus from the dead and seated Him at Your [own] right hand in the heavenly [places] (see Ephesians 1:17–20 AMPC).

[God] grant me out of the rich treasury of Your glory to be strengthened and reinforced with mighty power in my inner man by the [Holy] Spirit [Himself indwelling my innermost being and personality]. May Messiah through my faith [actually] dwell (settle down, abide, make Your permanent home) in my heart! May I be rooted deep in [Your] love and founded securely on [Your] love, that I may have the power and be strong to apprehend and grasp...[the experience of that love] [and know] the breadth and length and height and depth [of it]; [that I may really come] to know [practically, through experience for myself] the love of Messiah, which far surpasses mere knowledge [without experience]; that I may be filled [through all my being] unto all the fullness of God [may I have the richest measure of Your divine Presence, and become a body wholly filled and flooded with God Himself]! (See Ephesians 3:16–19 AMPC.)

[God] [You] disarmed the principalities and powers that were ranged against me and made a bold display and public example of them [open shame] in triumphing over them in Him and in it [the cross defeated them. Now

that Jesus has dethroned them I can rule over them] (see Colossians 2:15 AMPC).

[My Father] has delivered and drawn me to Himself out of the control and the dominion of darkness and has transferred me into the kingdom of the Son of His love (see Colossians 1:13 AMPC).

Whatever I forbid [command] and declare to be improper and unlawful on earth must be what is already forbidden in heaven, and whatever I permit and declare proper and lawful on earth must be what is already permitted in heaven. [I command the devil in Jesus' Name because of and to enforce my covenant rights] (see Matthew 18:18 AMPC).

*God has given me authority...to trample upon serpents and scorpions, and...over **all** the power that the enemy [possesses]; and **nothing** shall in any way harm me (see Luke 10:19 AMPC).*

I am strong in the Lord and in the power of His might. [He has granted me His authority/delegated power] (see Ephesians 6:10).

*He who is **in** me [Jesus] is greater than [the devil] (see 1 John 4:4).*

***All** authority has been given to Jesus in heaven and on earth. [And He said to me] go therefore (see Matthew 28:18-19).*

I demand my right in faith and am not moved by sense realm!

[God will grant me] whatever I ask [whatever I demand of the devil as my covenant rights and privileges] in Jesus' Name [as presenting all that I am], so that the Father may be glorified and extolled in the Son. [Yes] He will grant...whatever I shall ask [demand of the devil] in His Name [as presenting all that I am] (see John 14:13-14 AMPC).

*[God] raised Jesus from the dead and seated Him at His [own] right hand in the heavenly [places], far above **all** rule and authority and power and dominion and every name that is named [above every title that can be conferred], not only in this age and in this world, but also in the age and the world which are to come. And God has put **all** things under Jesus' feet and has appointed Jesus the universal and supreme **Head** of the **church** [His Body]* (see Ephesians 1:20-22 AMPC).

He raised me up together with Him and made me sit down together [giving me joint seating with Him] in the heavenly sphere [by virtue of my being] in Messiah Jesus. [I am seated with Jesus, in Him, as part of His Body in heavenly places. I am in two places at once. He is in me on earth and I am in Him in heaven] (see Ephesians 2:6 AMPC).

[I] resist the devil [stand firm against him] [by demanding he be bound and go to the feet of Jesus. I am in His Body, so that makes the devil under my feet too] and he will flee [run as in terror] from me (see James 4:7).

Note

1. Mayo Clinic Staff, "Kleptomania," Mayo Clinic, November 11, 2014, http://www.mayoclinic.org/diseases-conditions/kleptomania/basics/definition/con-20033010.

Part Two

YOUR SUPERNATURAL TOOLS

If I sat down with you and provided one-on-one mentorship in the supernatural, we could talk forever! Over four decades, I have gleaned from the best of the best—men and women who have walked in unusual realms of the Spirit, where they demonstrated supernatural power comparable to what we read about in the Scriptures. Perhaps the most notable to me was Kathryn Kuhlman, as mentioned in my Introduction.

And yet, if we only had a limited time to talk, there are three supernatural tools I would teach you about that are essential to you fulfilling the God assignment on your life.

First, you need to have *stubborn faith*. In our world today, people don't know how to be unwavering. We are so accustomed to getting what we want, *when* we want it, that if things don't instantly work out the way we expect, we give up. This is not faith. The faith God has entrusted to you can outlast any storm. In fact, the faith you received is a gift straight from God and it is a catalyst through which you can access the supernatural power of heaven and bring it right into your world today.

Second, you need to pray and believe for *supernatural healing*. Divine healing is not a secondary matter. When someone is healed of a physical disease, emotional pain, trauma, or even demonic torment, that healing is a sign and wonder that reveals that the superior Kingdom of God has broken into the world and has superimposed itself over the powers of darkness. Healing is a physical, visible sign that the Kingdom of God is advancing, that Jesus has authority over all things, and that the Messiah is resurrected and alive! Because so many are sick and hurting, I've provided a list of popular *healing questions and answers* that will help you navigate through some of the toughest concerns people have about supernatural healing and miracles.

Third and finally, you need to activate your *supernatural languages*. Perhaps more than divine healing, *speaking in tongues* has been a biblical truth that has been under assault since the early 1900s and the birth of classical Pentecostalism. The wonderful news is that every believer in Messiah can operate in this amazing gift!

I pray that as you study these three supernatural tools, you will be activated to step out and start watching the power of God flow through your life.

Chapter 4

YOUR STUBBORN FAITH

But without faith it is impossible to please Him, for he who comes to God must believe that He is, and that He is a rewarder of those who diligently seek Him.

—Hebrews 11:6

The Bible says that without faith you can't please God. I want to be a God-pleaser, don't you? Everything in His Kingdom is accessed through faith. Most believers think they understand faith, and yet most have not received all that God has provided for them. They read the promises in the Bible, but they don't see the supernatural in their lives. If that's you, I want to mentor you on how to operate in faith by speaking the language of heaven.

Steps to Walking in Miracle-Working Faith

I want to share a few keys to walking in miracle-working faith. This ability is not just available to a select few. Every believer in Messiah Jesus can operate in a measure of faith that releases the miraculous.

First, we have to *"receive the Kingdom of God like a child"* (Luke 18:17 NLT). Imagine a father in a swimming pool reaching out to his three-year-old child standing at the edge. The father says, "Jump!" Now the little child doesn't even have a thought of being afraid. He trusts his father's love and protection and jumps. The father, in turn, is there to catch him. That's childlike faith. It's time for us to jump into the arms of our loving Father. I pray in Yeshua's name that the spiritual scales and the hurts and the disappointments you have experienced will be completely removed and you will become as a little child, totally believing the words of your heavenly Father.

Victory does not come through overanalysis of what God is asking you to do; it comes through obedience to what He is saying.

Second, we need to be reminded of Messiah Jesus' teaching that *"the thief* [satan] *does not come except to steal, and to kill, and to destroy. I have come that they may have life, and that they may have it more abundantly"* (John 10:10). There are different Greek words for "life." The one used in this passage is *zoe*, which means "the life of God." It's not just your natural life. Messiah has come that you should have the life of God and that it should be "abundant" in your life.

These seem like two very simple steps, but the truth is they are often very misunderstood and, thereby, misapplied in many believers' lives. Instead of receiving the Kingdom like a child and expressing childlike trust in a good Father, we overcomplicate things. We operate from natural thinking instead of a renewed mind. God tells us to "jump," and instead we give Him every excuse as to why the jump is not logical. It doesn't make sense. It doesn't add up. It doesn't compute. All the symptoms in my body shout, "I am *not* healed! I have prayed in the past with no results." There is a new move of God and a new beginning for you. Victory does not come through overanalysis of what God is asking you to do; it comes through obedience to what He is saying.

Also, there are many believers who are simply not aware of the enemy's agenda against them. If Jesus really meant that we could enjoy abundant life, then our aim should be to resist any barrier that tries to keep us from experiencing this promise. The problem is that many people are not aware of the presence of the devil and his demons. At best, they believe in the devil but don't talk about him; at worst, they choose not to believe in him at all. I am not talking about unbelievers now; I am talking about followers of Jesus! I am talking about those who have become so secularized in their thinking that any traces of the supernatural, spiritual warfare, angels, and demons are considered irrational.

The one who denies the devil will easily accept defeat by the devil.

Whether it sounds rational or not, Jesus spoke about a thief who wars against you walking in abundant life. Saying that the devil is irrational or nonexistent will not stop his attacks. If anything, denying the devil gives him more opportunity for victory because the one who denies the devil will easily accept defeat by the devil. The horrible truth is, when they don't believe in the devil they consider their defeat, their sickness, and their oppression the result of "God's will." No! Jesus made it clear that God's will is abundant life and that the thief (the devil) is the author of everything that opposes abundance. Jesus made it abundantly clear: *"The thief does not come except to steal, and to kill, and to destroy"* (John 10:10).

Faith to Unlock Your Inheritance of Abundant Life

Abundant life is your inheritance. However, the statement Jesus made in John 10:10 explains that the reality of you walking in the full, abundant life of heaven has an enemy. The thief, the devil, does not want you accessing this *zoe* life. Why? Your abundance means his destruction. You walking in the fullness of God, by default, destroys the works of the devil.

First John 3:8 says, *"The reason the Son of God was made manifest (visible), was to undo (destroy, loosen, and dissolve) the works the devil [has done]"* (AMPC). That's Messiah's purpose. He came to earth to do this, and now you have been filled with the same anointing that Jesus had, to do the same works He did (see John 14:12)! You have access to the same Holy Spirit who anointed the Son of God. You too can draw upon His supernatural power to unlock the abundant life of heaven here and now!

Here is the problem that every single person faces, believer and unbeliever. The devil has his target directed at humanity. The devil hates all people because they are created in the image of God. All human beings have access to a realm of authority superior to the devil. Those who receive salvation through Messiah Jesus actually step into this realm of abundant life. It's a life with divine advantage. It's a life where we have been given authority to shut down torment that comes against us. It's a life where we cancel assignments of fear, death, and oppression. It's a life where sickness does not need to be tolerated and accepted. It's a life of unlimited access to the holy presence of God.

This is the life that every single believer in the Messiah is called to walk in and enjoy. *So what's the problem?* We live by feelings, not faith. We respond to the circumstances of life using human rationality, not the supernatural strategies of God.

You need to be convinced that God is the life-giver and the devil is the life-taker! You must learn to differentiate what comes from heaven and, likewise, what comes from hell. Only then will you be armed to accept God's will and reject the devil's. When you recognize that the devil has strategies that he uses against you, you will stand on God's Word with a stubborn, unrelenting faith. In other words, you will not back down and you will not give up until God's promises come to pass—in spite of what opposition is coming against you. Stubborn faith demands two things from you—resistance and persistence.

> Messiah Jesus was beaten and broken so you could walk in wholeness. Healing is your covenant from God.

Stubborn Faith Resists and Persists

You need to resist the devil and you need to persist in faith!

Resist the devil. I love the Wuest translation of James 4:7: *"Be subject with implicit [without doubt and unquestioning] obedience to God at once and once for all. Stand immovable against the onset of the devil and he will flee [as in terror]."*

How long should you resist the plans of the enemy? Until the sickness flees from you! But be encouraged—every time you resist by praying in tongues, the spirit of infirmity gets weaker. Every time you resist by speaking out loud about the blood of Jesus, it gets weaker. Every time you declare out loud the promises of God, it gets weaker. Every time you take communion, the demon behind the sickness is weaker.

This book is designed to equip you with practical, powerful tools to help you resist the enemy and persist to experience supernatural breakthrough. I mentioned a few things above that we will more fully discuss in later chapters, namely your supernatural language and healing Scriptures. For now, just know that God has tools that He wants to equip you with to resist the attacks of the devil.

Persist in faith. On multiple occasions in the Gospels, Jesus encouraged His disciples (and those listening to His teaching) to persist in prayer. He never gives instruction to back down and tolerate demonic torment. Look at both Luke 18:1–8 and Matthew 7:7–12. These are two examples of persistent faith. Keep speaking to your body that is afflicted and demand the spirit of infirmity leave and command your body to be whole. This is why Jesus died!

When disease comes against you, you need to persistently stand on the Word of God for healing until your sickness comes into agreement with what God says—and God's word on the matter is healing and wholeness. When the enemy comes to torment you through unrest, confusion, emotional pain, trauma, etc., you need to persistently believe that God's will for you is wholeness. Messiah Jesus was beaten and broken so you could walk in wholeness. Healing is your covenant from God.

The enemy of persistence is lack of results. People stop persisting in faith because, in the natural, they don't see any visible shifts in their circumstances. They don't witness immediate changes, developments, or turnaround. As a result, we have been programmed to accept our circumstances as God's will. This kills the flow of faith. Faith will flow only as far as there is hope, for the Bible talks about how faith and hope work together. Faith believes for what hope reveals.

The author of Hebrews writes this, describing faith: *"Now faith is the substance of things hoped for, the evidence of things not seen"* (Heb. 11:1). Don't let the lack of immediate results steal your hope. Keep your hope grounded in the Word of God. Every promise should fuel your hope. Every testimony of God's faithfulness is a reminder to you to keep persisting in faith. Keep believing. This does not just automatically happen, though. Don't expect to persist in faith naturally. It is not natural; it is supernatural. Your ability to continue believing God in spite of circumstances, in spite of feelings, in spite of your senses, and even in spite of things looking like they are getting worse comes through the supernatural power of the Holy Spirit. Keep demanding your body get in line with His promises. Never give up! A wise man said, "God's Word says it; I believe it; that settles it!"

Steadfast, Stubborn Faith Is Your Key to the Supernatural Lifestyle

Keep persisting in faith and continue to believe God, and you will see miracles. It's not rocket science! Those who stay the course always see more miracles than those who give up. This is because those who give up simply don't exercise their faith anymore to see the miraculous. Faith and the miraculous are vitally linked together. While I believe that God can and will do miracles sovereignly, the Bible standard is that a demonstration of faith activates the miraculous. I refuse to put God in a box. At the same time, I also refuse to neglect the principles that are clearly outlined in Scripture.

 Faith should be your first language.

Listen as Jesus speaks to you personally right now: *"I assure you, most solemnly I tell you, if anyone steadfastly believes in Me, he himself will be able to do the things that I do; and he will do even greater things than these, because I go to the Father"* (John 14:12 AMPC). So you're supposed to do at least what the Messiah did. What did Jesus do?

He raised the dead and healed the blind, the deaf, and the lame. These are all normal if you speak the heavenly language of faith. It's so simple, you need tradition and the devil to get confused.

God's Law of Attraction

Now that you understand the importance of having stubborn, persistent faith, I want to explain why the language of faith is essential. As a believer, faith should be your first language. It should impact everything about your life—especially how you speak. Unfortunately, there are many followers of Messiah who profess Jesus with their lips, but the majority of what comes out of their mouths attracts the powers of darkness.

You can position yourself to attract angels or the demonic. When you speak negative words or gossip or just repeat the bad things you have heard on the evening news, you attract the demonic. You are inviting the devil into your environment by agreeing with what he is doing, either in your life or in the world at large. Listening to that kind of negativity is just as bad. It is poison. Remember, what comes out of your mouth is the overflow of what's on the inside (see Luke 6:45).

What happens when you are exposed to negativity? After all, our world is filled with it. What happens when you are bombarded with bad news on the television, newspaper, or social media? You need to make a choice. Instead of speaking out the negative, you need to declare, in faith, what God is doing. You need to keep your words in alignment with God's words. It doesn't mean you pretend problems away; instead, it means your agreement is with God, no matter what you see and experience in life.

When you speak negative things, you attract the opponents to faith—the devil and his demons. When you speak positive things from the Scriptures, however, you attract angels, the Holy Spirit, Jesus, and Father God! Who do you want to attract?

Speaking words of life releases His presence. Wherever you go, people will want to be in your presence. People will feel good when you are near them and people will get healed and delivered by being near you. Why? Your words attract blessing. They attract angels. They create an atmosphere of faith where others can actually experience a taste of what you are filled with.

What must you do to cultivate this awesome presence of God as the atmosphere around you? Pray in tongues, read the Bible, worship God, confess God's Word out loud, and refuse negativity. Do everything possible to release your stubborn faith through these supernatural tools that God has given you!

> Speaking words of life releases His presence. They attract angels. They create an atmosphere of faith where others can actually experience a taste of what you are filled with.

Just Take It!

Stubborn faith receives what has been made available through the covenant promises of God! What keeps us from accessing these promises? It's not a lack of faith—it's a lack of knowledge. Before faith, we need to have hope. Before hope, we need to have knowledge.

In Hosea 4:6, we read why the people of God were being destroyed: *"My people are destroyed for lack of knowledge."* We are destroyed not because of a lack of faith, but because we do not *know* what covenantal blessings and privileges have been made available to us. Faith lays hold of promises. It sounds simple, *just take it*, but what keeps people from taking what belongs to them is lack of knowledge of the *"great and precious promises"* that God has provided (2 Pet. 1:4 NLT).

For example, our healing was granted to us in a covenant from God. The healing covenant and the remission of sin covenant happened in the invisible world when Messiah died for us. This was prophesied 800 years before Messiah came to earth. Isaiah writes, *"Surely He* [Messiah] *has borne our griefs and carried our sorrows"* (Isa. 53:4). The word for "borne" in the Hebrew is *nasa'*, which means "to be taken away." On Yom Kippur, the Day of Atonement, the high priest would put his hand on the scapegoat and deposit the sins of the Jewish people and the scapegoat would bear (*nasa'*) them away. They even went so far as to push the scapegoat over a cliff so no one would ever see those sins again.

In the Hebrew, the word for "griefs" means "sicknesses." Jesus took your sicknesses to a place where you'll never see them again. He carried your sorrows. You know what the word for "sorrows" means in the Hebrew? Your "pains." He took your pains, so why should you take them? Your sickness and pain is pushed over the cliff, never to be seen again.

> How are you going to be empowered? You are going to give praise and glory to God.

Peter is looking back at that great event when he says, *"by whose* [Messiah's] *stripes you were healed"* (1 Pet. 2:24). Our language of faith is a heavenly language in a zone where there is no time. There is just now. Everything is now. *"By whose stripes you were healed"*— now! Have you ever pleaded, "Oh Jesus, please heal me"? If you could hear the assembly in heaven answering you, they would be saying, "He already did it. Just take it!"

When I interviewed Dave Hayes, known as the "Praying Medic," he shared about how he prays for people in the ambulance as they are rushed to the hospital. He reached a point of seeing 80 percent healed! Dave teaches that "our victory comes from what Jesus has already done. All we do is inform the world the victory has already been won!"

Faith Is the Title Deed

The best definition of true faith is found in Hebrews 11:1: *"Now faith is the title deed of things hoped for"* (Wuest). When you have the deed to your home, it's yours. It's a done deal. Faith is your title deed to the promises of God. It's your evidence. Doubting Thomas wanted to see Jesus' wounds before he would believe that the Messiah had been raised from the dead. Jesus replied, *"Thomas, because you have seen Me, you have believed. Blessed are those who have not seen and yet have believed"* (John 20:29). In other words, "Blessed are those who just take My evidence, who will take the title deed without seeing." The Word of God is all the proof you need!

In Romans 4, Paul talks about the faith of Abraham. God said to Abraham, *"As it is written, 'I have made you a father of many nations'"* (Rom. 4:17). At that point Abraham didn't have a child through Sarah, but God was saying, *"I've made you the father of not just Isaac, but of many nations."* God speaks of the nonexistent things as if they already existed. That's the heavenly language. Faith is heaven's language because it sees from divine perspective, unrestrained by the hindrance of time. God can speak of the nonexistent things as though they already exist because of both His creative power and His omniscience. He is all powerful, so He can create the uncreated; but also, He can see into the future, the intended result that faith is purposed to release.

How does this apply to us? We need to follow God's example. Paul instructs the Ephesian church, *"Therefore be imitators of God, as beloved children"* (Eph. 5:1 ESV). Follow God's example and declare things that are not as though they were (see Rom. 4:17). We need to speak it even though we don't see it. How did Abraham faithfully do this, even when he did not see instant manifestation? After all, the great patriarch of the faith was given an enormous promise—he would be given a son from his own body—when he was long past the age to father children, and likewise his wife was long past the age of childbearing. Maybe you can relate. In the natural, things look dead. They look hopeless. Your circumstance is like a mountain that you cannot move, no matter how hard you try. You're praying. You're declaring. You're confessing. You're believing. And still, nothing seems to be happening. What do you do?

Consider that Abraham *"did not weaken in faith when he considered the [utter] impotence of his own body, which was as good as dead because he was about a hundred years old, or [when he considered] the barrenness of Sarah's [deadened] womb. No unbelief or distrust made him waver (doubtingly question) concerning the promise of God, but he grew strong and was empowered by faith as he gave praise and glory to God"* (Rom. 4:19-20 AMPC).

Activate your faith by boldly declaring that there is nothing too hard for the Lord!

How was Abraham empowered by God to remain stubborn in faith? He gave praise and glory to God. How are you going to be empowered? You are going to give praise and glory to God. This is so simple. Abraham was fully satisfied and assured that God was able and mighty to do what He said and to keep His promise. Praise helps us magnify God. No amount of words, declarations, or songs of praise from earth can increase the size of the One in heaven. When the Bible talks about magnifying the Lord, it's not that human beings have the ability to make God bigger. Rather, to magnify the Lord is to see Him as He really is. If anything needs to increase, it's not the size of God—it's how we *see* the size of God when compared to our problems. Even the tallest mountain is but a speck of dust when measured beside the expansiveness of our God. Abraham's faith could only go as far as His image of God. The same is true for you. If you don't see God as Almighty and all powerful, able to do anything, then you will weaken in faith.

Is Anything Too Hard for the Lord?

Remember what happened when God told Abraham and Sarah that they would have a child?

> *And He said, "I will certainly return to you according to the time of life, and behold, Sarah your wife shall have a son." (Sarah was listening in the tent door which was behind him.) Now Abraham and Sarah were old, well advanced in age; and Sarah had passed the age of child-bearing. Therefore Sarah laughed within herself, saying, "After I have grown old, shall I have pleasure, my lord being old also?" And the Lord said to Abraham, "Why did Sarah laugh, saying, 'Shall I surely bear a child, since I am old?' Is anything too hard for the Lord? At the appointed time I will return to you, according to the time of life, and Sarah shall have a son"* (Genesis 18:10-14).

When God reminded Abraham that he and Sarah would have a son, Sarah overheard and laughed. Why? It sounded unbelievable, especially because Abraham and Sarah had already tried in their natural, human strength to fulfill God's promise. In turn, they got Ishmael. Faith simply believes God; it does not try to manufacture His promised outcome. We lean on the Lord, trusting Him to accomplish what we are powerless to bring forth through our own efforts. The whole point of faith is to trust completely in the Lord with childlike abandon, believing that He will bring His promises to pass. We do this regardless of how laughable His promises sound to our natural ears.

Even though the odds were clearly against Abraham and Sarah—both of them were advanced in age and Sarah was past the age of childbearing—God was inviting them into the faith factor. Faith can trump natural odds because faith attracts the miracle-working power of God into impossibilities. Faith literally draws God into a situation that has no natural remedy and He turns it around for His glory.

God invited Abraham and Sarah into the supernatural dimension of faith, asking the rhetorical question: *"Is anything too hard for the Lord?"* (Gen. 18:14). The answer is obvious: *No, nothing is impossible for God!* Yet God was reminding Abraham and Sarah of this truth so He could invite them into faith activation.

When Abraham gave praise and glory to God, he was constantly reminding himself of the God who could do all things. I encourage you to activate your faith by boldly declaring that there is nothing too hard for the Lord!

When you pray and believe, you could receive a healing, which is a gradual miracle, or a miracle, which is an instant healing.

The Difference between Miracles and Healings

In Luke 13:18-19, Jesus tells us *"the kingdom of God...is like a mustard seed, which a man took and put in his garden; and it grew and became a large tree."* The Word of God is a seed. You speak the Word of God and you plant that seed. In the natural, if you plant a seed you don't go out the next day and dig it up, because there is no chance that seed is going to take root and grow. The way you dig up the seed spiritually is to speak the negative language of earth about your situation rather than your heavenly language of faith. This is one way you activate faith—through your words. Your words represent the action of faith.

Remember, the Bible says that faith without a corresponding action is dead (see James 2:17 NIV). I often wondered why Jesus cursed two different fig trees, and then God gave me a revelation. The first time He cursed a fig tree, nothing appeared to happen, but the next day it *"dried up from the roots"* (see Mark 11:12–14, 20-21). If you had been there the first day, you might have said, "Jesus messed up big time—I heard Him curse the fig tree but it's still alive." But Jesus' word was working in the invisible world under the soil. The roots were withered. He had an impact when He spoke, but the results were not visible right away. That's an example of God's promises come to fruition. You have an impact when you speak in faith, declaring the Word of God, but the results might not be immediately visible. Don't let that discourage you. Keep exercising and working out your faith, even if you don't see instant breakthrough. Trust that there is movement taking place in the invisible realm. The progressive nature of what we see illustrated in this fig tree scenario represents a healing.

The next time Jesus cursed a fig tree, it died immediately (see Matt. 21:19). That is an example of a miracle. When you pray and believe, you could receive a healing, which is a gradual miracle, or a miracle, which is an instant healing. Many people, when they don't get a miracle, give up on their healing or breakthrough. Today, we want everything instantly. But God wants you to start operating like Him. You're a heavenly creation. You're in this world but you're not of this world. You've received enough of His Word to know how to receive from God. Now make up your mind that you're a heavenly being, and when you pray you're either going to get a healing or a miracle. This stubborn approach fuels your persistence.

Speak to Your Mountain

Jesus said, *"Truly I say to you that whoever would say to this mountain…."* So when you are praying, speak directly to the mountain or to the problem. *"Whoever would say to this mountain, 'You must immediately be removed and you must immediately be cast into the sea,' and would not doubt in his heart but would believe that what he is saying is happening, it will be to him…whatever you are asking, believe that you have taken it, and it will be there for you"* (Mark 11:23-24 The One New Man Bible). I like that word *taken. Grab it! Take it!*

Some don't speak the Word and some don't have an action. You need both. Speak to your mountain and command it in the name of Jesus to immediately leave. If you are going by what you see, you're in the wrong realm.

Let's put this into practice. For example, if you have any sickness in your body, I want you to *command* it (the spirit of infirmity) to leave. It's not from God. It's preventing you from walking in abundant life. You belong to Jesus. His blood covered your sickness and disease. With these truths in mind, you need to operate *commanding* power through faith. You are not commanding God. God has already made the "command" by making it clear in the Word. You are speaking to the mountain; you are commanding the problem to come into agreement with God's promise. Not only do you command the spirit of infirmity to leave, but you speak to your body and command it to line up with the Word of God.

Peter reminds us that *by His stripes you were healed*. This promise is past tense. I want you to command the sickness that's afflicting you to leave and command healing to come in Jesus' name. You actually have commanding power in the spirit realm through faith. You can't be wishy-washy. You can't be indecisive. Faith is not maybe; faith is *now*. Faith enforces the victory that Jesus the Messiah won on the cross. He doesn't need to win the victory; He already did it! Your healing is past tense. Your breakthrough has been purchased. Your blessing has been secured. You need to speak, command, and declare the things that are not as though they are. I repeat, be stubborn in your faith!

Next, I want you to *take* your healing with thanksgiving. If you don't see anything happen, then you're blessed. Jesus said, *"Blessed are those who have not seen and yet have believed"* (John 20:29). This is the heavenly language of faith—being able to believe that something happened even though we see no natural evidence of it happening yet. Remember, just because you don't see anything changing immediately doesn't mean your faith was ineffective. Now is a good time to use your sanctified imagination. Imagine you are healed. Thank God for that healing. Your body must line up with God's Word!

If you don't dig up the seed, your healings will turn into miracles.

Did you receive a *miracle* or a *healing?* Test it out. If it was a back problem, bend over. If it was a knee problem, bend your knee. If it was a neck problem, move your neck around. God says faith without a corresponding action is dead. You don't have dead faith, right? Then I encourage you to do something that you couldn't do previously.

If you had a symptom and it's gone now, you had a miracle. If the symptom is still there, you received a healing. You see where people get faked out? When they don't get the miracle, they say, "I guess it didn't work for me." No more! You're speaking the heavenly language from now on.

What to Do When Your Faith Is Tested

So many times I'll pray for people and they get healed, but later when they walk out of the presence of that heavenly atmosphere the devil tests them and they give up. They say, "I *was* healed, but the symptom came back." When I was a brand-new believer, I met a man who was supernaturally healed so that he could see without glasses for the first time in his remembrance. The next day, he needed his glasses again. He came to me to find out why. At that time, I didn't know the answer. Now I know. When the miracle occurs, the devil has to leave under the presence of God. Then he comes back and tests you for the Word's sake. Just declare, "You get off me, pain! You don't belong here. I am healed. You hear that? I am healed in Jesus' name. Go! Go!" Be stubborn. If you don't dig up the seed, your healings will turn into miracles.

Finally, don't let any of this become a legalistic formula. Instead, focus on developing a loving intimacy with your heavenly Father. As you seek God first and consciously determine to walk in His presence and love, watch His miracle-working power explode in your life! Faith is not a formula; it is the result of cultivating a lifestyle of closeness with God. When you know His character and nature, your faith will operate with greater force.

For I Have Chosen You

The Haggai principle is a great lesson on stubborn faith. The prophet Haggai exhorted the returned Jewish exiles to resume the rebuilding of the Temple. As they started to build, it looked like "nothing" in comparison to the former Temple (see Hag. 2:3).

But Haggai had faith for the future Temple of which the one they rebuilt was only a shadow. The future Temple was the Holy Spirit dwelling in our physical bodies.

When this would happen, there would be a major change. Instead of *"you have planted much but harvest little"* (Hag. 1:6 NLT), God promises even *"while the seed is still in the barn...from this day onward I will bless you"* (Hag. 2:19 NLT). Did you get that? The seed was not yet planted, but God guaranteed they would be blessed. This is God's Word for you today. *From this day onward I will bless you!*

Like Haggai, I do not look at the way it used to be. I look at the promises that are available now! This is God's promise to you:

> *I will shake all the nations, and the **treasures** of all the nations will be brought to this Temple. I will **fill this place with glory**....The **future glory** of this Temple will be **greater** than its **past glory**...And in this place I will bring **peace*** (Haggai 2:7,9 NLT).

The people who were reconstructing the Temple kept looking back to the previous glory. That is not faith. God promised in Haggai that He would start answering your prayers quickly. In fact, He promised your prayers would be answered before the seed (the promises) enter the ground. He promised the heathen would bring their treasures to you. He promised you would be filled with a greater glory than was even in the Temple. And He promised you would walk in supernatural peace. I believe this will be 24/7 peace.

Fasten your seat belt for the greatest move of God's Spirit in history. God says, "*for I have chosen you*" (Hag. 2:23).

Even our prayers will be answered instantly in this new season. In the next chapter, I will teach you how to meditate on my favorite healing Scriptures. Second Corinthians 4:13 says, "*I believed and therefore I spoke.*" Many people speak before they believe. By meditating on the promises you too will believe, speak it, and walk in your healing!

Chapter 5

YOUR HEALING SCRIPTURES (PROMISES)

I am the Lord that healeth thee.

—Exodus 15:26 KJV

How to Be Normal

Healing and faith are normal according to the Bible. Every believer has received faith; this faith has the ability to access miracles—including healing! We just learned about how we should exercise a *stubborn* and relentless faith. I want to specifically help you apply this faith to receive healing. If we truly want to model our lives after the Messiah, then we need to deal with sickness the same way He did—He healed *"all who were oppressed by the devil."* This is where we are headed!

> *God anointed Jesus of Nazareth with the Holy Spirit and with power, who went about doing good and **healing all who were oppressed by the devil**, for God was with Him* (Acts 10:38).

Look at Jesus' instructions for the ministries of healing and deliverance in the Gospels.

> *And as you go, preach, saying, "The kingdom of heaven is at hand." Heal the sick, cleanse the lepers, raise the dead, cast out demons* (Matthew 10:7-8).

What does *"the Kingdom of heaven is at hand"* look like? Healing. Deliverance. The dead being raised. The supernatural of God is a sign that the superior Kingdom of God has broken into the world through the power and presence of the Holy Spirit.

Even more specifically, Jesus describes divine healing in the same context of preaching the Kingdom of God.

> *And heal the sick there, and say to them, "The kingdom of God has come near to you"* (Luke 10:9).

Healing shows that the Kingdom of God has *come near*. God is not distant or detached from society. Even some believers have this cosmic clockmaker view of God, where He "wound everything up" with Creation and simply let it go, refusing to be involved in its affairs. This is a deception that we believe because of our lack of experience with the supernatural.

The supernatural is important. Divine healing is important. Do you know why? It's not simply about our bodies getting well and us being able to go back to life as "normal." Healing is so important because as God's supernatural power touches the sick and brings wholeness, people are reminded that God is not distant—He is near. The proof is in His healing power. A "god" who is a detached deity does not stoop down to bring a healing touch to those in need; this is simply not our God. He is involved. He sees and loves people. He reaches into their sickness with His healing touch, not just to help them feel better but to demonstrate that He is alive and active in the world. Healing reminds us all that God is alive, His Kingdom is near, and that we are ultimately accountable to Him. It's one thing to be accountable to a concept—a God who might be out there, somewhere, in outer space. It's another thing to be accountable to a Person who demonstrates His power. But even more important, "healings" are God's dinner bell to grab the attention of the unsaved and cause them to open up to the Gospel. This is why healing and the supernatural are so important and why I want to mentor you in how to activate your faith to see miracles and healings.

> Healing is so important because as God's supernatural power touches the sick and brings wholeness, people are reminded that God is not distant—He is near.

Faith: The Key to Experiencing Heaven's Reward

Hebrews 11:6 tells us, *"But without faith it is impossible to please Him, for he who comes to God must believe that He is, and that He is a rewarder of those who diligently seek Him."*

I started my own research into the subjects of healing and faith over 40 years ago. Where did I begin? Studying the Scriptures. It didn't take long before I was overwhelmed by the fact that it is God's will to heal sickness and disease.

- First, I listed all the faith and healing Scriptures I could find.

- I followed by personalizing the verses.

- Finally, I started meditating on them.

This discovery helped me create a Bible-based blueprint that will help you practically experience the supernatural healing power of God in your life.

I recently spoke to an Orthodox Jewish woman who became a believer in Jesus through one of my Jewish evangelistic books, *They Thought for Themselves*. Her only teaching was our television show, *It's Supernatural!* She was shocked when I told her some Christians believe healing stopped when the apostles died.

Miracles have not stopped, God still heals today, and the same Jesus who walked the earth healing *all* who were oppressed by the devil wants to release His power through you!

I want to share an ancient secret in this chapter that will help you activate your faith—where the Bible goes from information to revelation. You were never meant to simply read the Bible or study its pages; you were meant to put Scripture to work and see supernatural results. *What's the key?* Biblical meditation.

Faith and healing will no longer be a mystery!

Your Revelation Starts Now!

This chapter includes my personal list of healing Scriptures for you to meditate on and speak out loud. As you meditate on these promises, they will begin to drop from your head to your heart. Revelation starts to take place. What used to be a thought in your mind is now becoming a belief system in your heart that completely changes the way you see and respond to sickness. You will begin to believe with all your heart that God's will is for you to be healed. Faith and healing will no longer be a mystery!

Simple Steps to Meditating on Scripture

*But his delight is in the law of the Lord, and in His law he **meditates** day and night* (Psalm 1:2).

Meditate in the Hebrew language means "to speak or mutter." Therefore, the Jewish way to meditate is to speak out loud the words of God.

When meditating on Scripture, I do the following:

1. Personalize the verse. Psalm 91:1 (Personalizing) *"He who dwells…"* (unpersonalized) becomes *"I dwell…"* (personalized).

2. Visualize yourself doing what the verse says.

3. Speak and declare the verse out loud.

4. Add descriptive wording. Psalm 91:1 (Descriptive Wording) *"I dwell (I actually breathe and live inhaling the rarefied air of heaven) in the secret place of the Most High."*

I like to compare meditation to eating steak. If you eat the steak in one gulp, not only will you not digest it, you will probably choke to death. But if you take a knife and fork and cut a small bite-size and chew it and then swallow it, it will be digested and become nourishment to your body. Stop making reading the Bible a speed contest. Start taking small bites and chew on them, meditating until the Word becomes flesh.

In the following pages, I am providing you with a categorized selection of Scriptures that you can meditate on and declare over all matters of sickness, disease, and infirmity. Remember, God wants His healing power to flow to you and through you.

Your Personalized Healing Scriptures

I Meditate on God's Word

I am strong and very courageous. I am careful to obey all the instructions; I do not deviate from them, turning either to the right or to the left. This is why I am successful in **everything** *I do. I study this Book of Instruction* **continually**. *I* **meditate** *on it* **day and night**. *Only then will I prosper and succeed in* **all** *I do* (see Joshua 1:7-8 NLT).

My faith comes by **hearing,** *and* **hearing** *by the* **Word** *of God. [When I hear myself speaking God's Word, my faith grows and I become a God pleaser]* (see Romans 10:17).

I am blessed because my delight is in the law of the Lord, and in His law do I meditate [ponder by talking to myself] day and night. I am like a tree planted by the rivers of water, that brings forth its fruit in its season, whose leaf also shall not wither; and whatever I do shall prosper (see Psalm 1:1-3).

I give **attention** *to God's words; I incline my* **ear** *to His sayings. I do not let them depart from my* **eyes;** *I keep them in the midst of my* **heart;** *for they are* **life** *and* **health** *to* **all** *my flesh* (see Proverbs 4:20-22).

*I **believed** and therefore I **spoke**, I also believe [because I meditate on God's Word day and night] and therefore speak* (see 2 Corinthians 4:13).

Whatever is true, whatever is worthy of reverence and is honorable and seemly, whatever is just, whatever is pure, whatever is lovely and lovable, whatever is kind and winsome and gracious, if there is any virtue and excellence, if there is anything worthy of praise, I think on and weigh and take account of these things [I fix my mind on them] [and not on the opposite!] (see Philippians 4:8 AMPC).

Because I wait on the Lord My strength is renewed; I shall mount up with wings like eagles, I shall run and not be weary, I shall walk and not faint (see Isaiah 40:31).

My Faith Is in the Lord

*Now, **without faith** it is **impossible** to **please Him** at all. For he who comes to God must of the necessity in the nature of the case believe that He exists, that He also becomes a **rewarder** of those who **diligently** seek Him out* (see Hebrews 11:6 Wuest).

*[If I would] say to this mountain, "You **must** immediately be removed and you **must** immediately be cast into the sea," and would not doubt in my heart but would believe that what I am saying is happening, **it will be to me.** I must continually pray for everything, then for whatever I am asking, I believe that I have **taken** it, and it **will** be there for me* (see Mark 11:23-24 The One New Man Bible).

*Now **faith** is the **assurance** (the confirmation, the title deed) of the things [I] hope for, being the **proof** of things [I] **do not see** and the **conviction** of their **reality** [my faith perceives as real fact what is not revealed to my senses] (see Hebrews 11:1 AMPC).*

Anything is possible if I believe (see Mark 9:23 NLT).

Through faith and patience I inherit the promises (see Hebrews 6:12).

For God has not given me a spirit of fear, but of power and of love and of a sound mind (see 2 Timothy 1:7).

You will keep me in perfect peace [completeness], because my mind is stayed on You (see Isaiah 26:3).

Jesus said to me, "Blessed are those who have not seen and yet have believed" [I am blessed because I believe before I see!] (see John 20:29).

I will be of good cheer; my faith has made me well (see Matthew 9:22).

My faith by itself, if it does not have works [corresponding action], is dead. I will show you my faith by my works [corresponding action] (see James 2:17-18).

For by grace I am saved [healed] through faith, and this is not from myself, it is the gift of God (see Ephesians 2:8 NET).

My God Is Good!

But You, O Lord, are a God full of compassion, and gracious, longsuffering and abundant in mercy and truth (Psalm 86:15).

*If I serve [Hebrew: "worship"] the Lord my God, He will bless my bread and my water. And He will **take sickness away** from the midst of me. He will **fulfill** the number of my days (see Exodus 23:25-26).*

*For **all** the promises of God in Him are **Yes**, and in Him Amen [so be it] (see 2 Corinthians 1:20).*

*Now to Him who is able to do exceedingly abundantly above all that I ask or think, according to the **power** that works **in me** (see Ephesians 3:20).*

The thief comes only in order to steal and kill and destroy [sickness is stealing, killing, and destroying]. Jesus came that I may have and enjoy life [health], and have it in abundance (to the full; till it overflows) (see John 10:10 AMPC).

For His divine power has bestowed upon me all things that [are requisite and suited] to life and godliness, through the [full, personal] knowledge of Him. [I know this because] He has bestowed on me His precious and exceedingly great promises (see 2 Peter 1:3-4 AMPC).

For as the rain comes down, and the snow from heaven, and do not return there, but water the earth, and make it bring forth and bud, that it may give seed to the sower and bread to the eater, so shall God's word be that goes forth from my mouth; it shall not return to me void, but it shall accomplish what He pleases, and it shall prosper in the thing for which He sent it. For I shall go out with joy, and be led out with peace [completeness/shalom in spirit, soul, and body] (see Isaiah 55:10-12).

The Lord my God is in the midst of me, a Mighty One, a Savior [Who saves]! He will rejoice over me with joy; He will rest [in silent satisfaction] and in His love He will be silent and make no mention [of past sins, or even recall them]; He will exult over me with singing (see Zephaniah 3:17 AMPC).

No good thing will the Lord God withhold from me because I walk uprightly (see Psalm 84:11).

*Jesus said: I assure you, most solemnly I tell you, that My Father will grant you whatever you ask in My Name [as presenting all that I AM]. [I] ask and **keep on asking** and I **will** receive, so that my joy (gladness, delight) may be full and complete* (see John 16:23-24 AMPC).

*If I confess my sins, He is faithful and just to forgive my sins and to cleanse me from **all** unrighteousness* (see 1 John 1:9).

*He who is **in me** is **greater** than he who is in the world* (see 1 John 4:4).

For if I forgive people their trespasses [their reckless and willful sins, leaving them, letting them go, and giving up resentment], my heavenly Father will also forgive me. But if I do not forgive others their trespasses [their reckless and willful sins, leaving them, letting them go, and giving up resentment], neither will my Father forgive me my trespasses. [Forgiveness is a requirement. It is not an emotion or a feeling but a decision. It is not based on their deserving forgiveness any more than I deserved forgiveness. This does not mean I must trust the person. They must earn my trust. I choose to live in instant forgiveness!] (see Matthew 6:14-15 AMPC).

Bless the Lord, you His angels, who excel in strength, **who do His word**, *heeding the voice of His word [His promises in my mouth]* (see Psalm 103:20).

For the Lord my God holds my right hand; the Lord says to me, Fear not; I will help you! (see Isaiah 41:13 AMPC)

The goodness of God endures continually (Psalm 52:1).

I Trust in the Lord

God...calls the things [He has promised] that are not in existence as being [already] in existence. ...And not being weak with respect to his faith, [Abraham] attentively considered his own body permanently dead, he being about one hundred years old, also the deadness of Sarah's womb. Moreover, in view of the **promise** *of God, he did not vacillate in the sphere of unbelief between two mutually exclusive expectations but was strengthened with respect to his faith, having given glory to God, and was* **fully persuaded** *that what He had* **promised with finality** *He was able also to do* (see Romans 4:17-21 Wuest).

Every word which I shall speak which has no legitimate work, which is inoperative and thus morally useless and unprofitable, I shall give account of at the day of judgment, for by my words I shall be justified, and by my words shall I be condemned. [Thank God for repentance and the blood of Jesus!] (see Matthew 12:36-37 Wuest).

I consider it wholly joyful whenever I am enveloped in or encounter trials of any sort or fall into various temptations. I am assured and understand that the trial and *proving of my faith bring out **endurance** and **stead-fastness** and **patience**. I let endurance and steadfastness and patience have full play and do a thorough work in me, so that I may be perfectly and fully developed [with no defects], lacking in nothing. I am blessed (happy, to be envied) [when I am] patient under trial and stand up under temptation, for when I have stood the test and been approved, I **will** receive [the victor's] crown of life which God has promised to me because I love Him* (see James 1:2–4,12 AMPC).

*The Spirit of Him who raised Jesus from the dead dwells **in me**, He who raised Messiah from the dead will also give **life** [healing] to my mortal body through His Spirit who dwells in me* (see Romans 8:11).

*Now this is the confidence that I have in Him, that if I ask anything according to His will, He hears me [sickness is not His will]. And if I **know** that He hears me, whatever I ask, I know that I have the petitions that I have asked of Him* (see 1 John 5:14-15).

As He is, so am I in this world. There is no fear in love; but perfect [mature] love casts out fear. He who fears has not been made perfect [mature] in love [the love of God trumps fear] (see 1 John 4:17-18).

And this is the eternal life, namely, that I might be having an experiential knowledge of You, the only genuine God, and of Him whom You sent, Jesus the Messiah. [Every benefit of God comes as a result of my developing great intimacy with Him] (see John 17:3 Wuest).

The Lord is my light and my salvation [healing, deliverance, protection]—so why should I be afraid? (see Psalm 27:1 NLT)

I do not fear, for the Lord my God Himself fights for me (see Deuteronomy 3:22).

[I] never take revenge. I leave that to the righteous anger of God (see Romans 12:19 NLT).

I Am Healed!

*Surely He **has** borne my griefs [Hebrew: "pains"] and carried [away] my sorrows [Hebrew: "sicknesses"] and by His stripes **I am healed** (see Isaiah 53:4-5).*

*God anointed Jesus of Nazareth with the Holy Spirit and with power, who went about doing **good** and **healing all** who were oppressed by the devil, for **God** was with Him. [I am anointed with the Holy Spirit and power. I do good by healing all who are oppressed by the devil, for God is with me] (see Acts 10:38).*

For this purpose the Son of God was manifested, that He might destroy the works of the devil [I am to destroy sickness by commanding it to leave in Jesus' name] (see 1 John 3:8).

And there was none feeble among His tribes [I am His family!] (see Psalm 105:37)

He sent His word and healed me, and delivered me (see Psalm 107:20).

God has highly exalted Jesus and given Him the name which is above every name. [Your disease has a name.

Now speak to that spirit of infirmity in Jesus' Name and it must leave. It will stay until it is sure you will not give up through weariness or unbelief] (see Philippians 2:9).

*Because I have made the Lord, who is my refuge, even the Most High, my dwelling place, no evil [sickness] shall befall me, nor shall any plague come near my dwelling. With **long life** God will satisfy me, and show me His salvation [healing]* (see Psalm 91:9-10,16).

*Bless the Lord, O my soul, and forget not all His benefits: who forgives all my iniquities, who **heals all my diseases*** (see Psalm 103:2-3).

*I shall be blessed above all peoples. And the Lord will take away from me **all** sickness* (see Deuteronomy 7:14-15).

As Jesus left the house, he was followed by two blind men. Jesus said to them, "Do you really believe I can do this?" They said, "Why, yes, Master!" He touched their eyes and said, "Become what you believe" [I am becoming what I believe!] (see Matthew 9:27-30 MSG).

Your kingdom come. Your will be done on earth as it is in heaven [there is no sickness in heaven] (see Matthew 6:10).

I shall not die, but live, and declare the works of the Lord (Psalm 118:17).

By whose stripes I was healed (see 1 Peter 2:24).

He sent His word and healed me (see Psalm 107:20).

If I diligently obey the voice of the Lord my God, to observe carefully all His commandments which He commands…God will set me high above all nations of the earth. And all these blessings shall come upon me and overtake me, because I obey the voice of the Lord my God. The Lord has already caused my enemies [sicknesses] who rise against me to be defeated before my face (see Deuteronomy 28:1-2,7).

Even in old age I will still produce fruit (see Psalm 92:14 NLT).

The Lord will sustain, refresh, and strengthen me on my bed of languishing [sickbed]; [He completely heals me from my illness] (see Psalm 41:3 AMPC).

In all things I am prospering, and I will be continually having good health just as my soul is prospering (see 3 John 1:2 Wuest).

My Kingdom Purpose

God has given me the **keys** *of the kingdom of heaven; and whatever I bind on earth [forbid to be done], shall have been already bound [forbidden to be done] in heaven; and whatever I loose on earth [permit to be done], shall have already been loosed in heaven [permitted to be done]. [Sickness is already forbidden in heaven, and in Jesus' name I forbid it* (name the specific condition) *in my body!]* (see Matthew 16:19 Wuest).

For He made Him who knew no sin to be sin for me, that I might become the righteousness of God in Him [I am the righteousness of God in Him!] (see 2 Corinthians 5:21).

No weapon [sickness is a weapon of the enemy] formed against me shall prosper. This is my heritage as a servant of the Lord (see Isaiah 54:17).

*And Jesus came and spoke saying, "**All** authority has been given to Me in heaven and on earth. Go therefore…" [I have been delegated this same authority to make disciples]* (see Matthew 28:18-19).

*Behold, I have been given the authority to advance by setting my foot upon snakes and scorpions, and over **all** the power of the enemy, and **nothing** will in any case harm me* (see Luke 10:19 Wuest).

*I do not repay evil for evil. I do not retaliate with insults when people insult me. Instead, I pay them back with a blessing. That is what God has called me to do, and **He will grant me His blessing*** (see 1 Peter 3:9 NLT).

I resist the devil [I stand firm against him], and he will flee from me [as in terror] (see James 4:7 AMPC).

*I will not get tired of doing what is good. At just the right time I will reap a harvest of blessing **if** I don't give up* (see Galatians 6:9 NLT).

The devil tries to snare me by the words of my mouth [I have put a guard on my mouth to agree with what God says] (see Proverbs 6:2).

*I **overcome** the devil [and his fruit of sickness] by the **blood** of the Lamb and by the word of my **testimony** [every time I take communion, I disable the hold of sickness progressively more and more]* (see Revelation 12:11).

[Jesus said] if I steadfastly believe in Him, I will be able to do the things that He does; and I will do even greater things than these (see John 14:12 AMPC).

I am patient and kind. I am not jealous or boastful or proud or rude. I do not demand my own way. I am not irritable, and I keep no record of being wronged. I do not rejoice about injustice but rejoice whenever the truth wins out. I never give up, never lose faith, I am always hopeful, and I endure through every circumstance. [I never fail!] (see 1 Corinthians 13:4–8 NLT)

And this commandment I have from Him, [namely], I am constantly loving God [believe it for all it means] and should constantly be also loving my brother (see 1 John 3:23 Wuest).

I should always pray and not lose heart (see Luke 18:1 NET).

The Spirit of the Lord is upon me, because he has anointed me. He has sent me to proclaim release to the captives and the regaining of sight to the blind, to set free those who are oppressed (see Luke 4:18 NET).

Chapter 6

YOUR HEALING QUESTIONS

In this chapter, I want to specifically address some of the most common questions about divine healing. This is important because what people believe about healing has been a roadblock for them walking in the supernatural power of God.

From my 40 years of experience, I want to share some of what I have learned through both observation and conversation.

The questions I address in this section are some of the most frequently asked when it comes to divine healing. I want to give you practical insight along with what the Bible says to help answer your own questions and the questions that others have about healing.

Q. *Does everyone have the gift of healing?*

A. Not everyone has the specific gift of healing. But according to Mark 16:18, every believer can *"lay hands on the sick, and they will recover."* Every follower of Messiah Jesus has received the same Holy Spirit; His presence within you is what qualifies you to lay your hands on the sick and see them recover.

Q. *What are the steps I should follow to receive the gift of healing?*

A. To receive the gift of healing, you should walk in holiness and intimacy with God, meditate on the healing Scriptures in this book, and ask God for the gift. God responds to those who ask Him for such gifts, as the Scripture instructs:

> *Pursue and seek to acquire [this] love [make it your aim, your great quest]; and earnestly desire and cultivate the spiritual endowments (gifts)* [to be used by believers for the benefit of the church] (1 Corinthians 14:1 AMPC).

Biblically, you can *earnestly desire* the gifts of the Spirit, which are listed in First Corinthians 12 and 14. It is important for you to also recognize that while there are certain individuals who have operated in a special gift of healing, also, the Holy Spirit can use you at any time to operate in what Paul calls the *"gifts of healings"* (1 Cor. 12:9). This is listed among the nine manifestational gifts of the Spirit described by Paul in First Corinthians 12. Believers should live in a state of readiness and expectation to be used by God at any time as the *gifts of healings*, along with all other gifts of the Spirit, can be manifested through the Holy Spirit as He so choses (see 1 Cor. 12:11). But we are living in an unusual time when God is pouring out His gifts in abundance. Ask, believe, and receive.

Also, lay hands on and pray for the sick often. The way the first disciples learned to walk in miracles was to watch what Jesus did and do the same thing. Find someone with the gift of healing and volunteer to "carry his or her bags." In other words, volunteer to help them so they can mentor you. But if you pray for the sick often enough, I believe the gift will drop on you.

Q. *Can I pray for my own healing or does someone else have to pray over me?*

A. Every believer can lay hands on the sick (see Mark 16:18), so that means you can lay hands on yourself. Follow the same steps you would for someone else—walk in holiness and intimacy with God and confess the healing Scriptures within this book over your life.

> The difference between a healing and a miracle is that a healing is a gradual miracle and a miracle is an instant healing.

Q. *Why are many miracles today not instantaneous or complete like Jesus' miracles were?*

A. Not every healing by Jesus was instantaneous. The Bible tells us how He prayed for a blind man twice in order for him to be healed (see Mark 8:25). Jesus promised we would do the same works He did and even greater (see John 14:12)!

We are entering a time in history when God will anoint us like Jesus and we will see the same works and greater. Don't be discouraged when you do not see an instantaneous miracle. Keep praying and having faith in God. God may manifest His power in the form of a healing rather than a miracle. The difference between a healing and a miracle is that a healing is a gradual miracle and a miracle is an instant healing.

Q. *Why are some people healed and others are not?*

A. There can be many reasons for why some people are healed and others are not. Sometimes the reason is as simple as not repenting of sin or unforgiveness.

Another reason is some falter in their faith based on symptoms. Sometimes people will just give up. But we are not called to judge. We are called to be believers and believe God for His healing power to be demonstrated. We are to trust God and not question with our limited understanding. We are responsible for what we know, not for what we do not know. I will invest my life believing God's promises. That's *my* job. Healing is God's.

Q. *Is there a specific way to pray in order to see healing miracles happen?*

A. Jesus prayed different ways in the Gospels. Let the Holy Spirit direct you. Meditate on the healing Scriptures found in this book. Lay hands on the sick and believe. Sometimes people are healed instantly through a miracle and sometimes they are healed gradually. Do not be moved by what you see, but be moved *only* by the Word of God. If you can go witnessing with a believer who sees miracles when they pray, this will help grow your gift.

There is a very quick solution for the person who asks, "How can I start seeing healing miracles happen?" It's simply this—*start praying*. Take risks. Step out of your comfort zone and pray for as many sick people as possible. Don't be discouraged by what you *don't* see; instead, keep pressing in for what you *do* see in the Word of God. This is what should keep you praying for the sick, even if you are not seeing natural results. The established truth of Scripture is that it is God's will to heal sickness and disease. Jesus is the model that we follow, and He healed all who were oppressed by the devil. You have been given this same commission. Go forth in boldness, faith, and persistence—pray for healing and keep praying, and lay your hands on the sick until you begin to see the kind of miraculous results that the Bible promises.

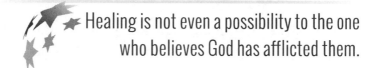

Healing is not even a possibility to the one who believes God has afflicted them.

Q. *Does God ever cause someone to get sick?*

A. God does not cause someone to get sick. However, sin, curses, or inherited (generational) curses open the door for the devil to put sickness on us. Thankfully, Galatians 3:13 says, "[Messiah] *has redeemed us from the curse of the law, having become a curse for us (for it is written, 'Cursed is everyone who hangs on a tree').*" Therefore, we can break curses through prayer. No matter how sickness comes, Jesus died for all of our diseases (see Ps. 103:3). Disease does not come from God. Killing, stealing, and destroying is the work of the devil whereas abundant life comes from God (see John 10:10).

This is a very important truth to communicate to people who are sick. If they believe that God is responsible for their sickness, this shuts down their ability to even have *hope* for a miracle, let alone faith to *receive* the miracle. Healing is not even a possibility to the one who believes God has afflicted them.

On the contrary, truth about God being the author of abundant life begins to create expectation for healing. This is why the healing Scriptures are so important. Every truth in the Bible that speaks to God's will for healing demolishes the lie that God actually afflicts people with sickness. Sickness does not come from God—it did not originate with Him. Sickness is a result of the fall. It was only introduced into the equation once Adam and Eve ate of the forbidden fruit, having believed the devil's lie.

Q. *Can God heal more than just physical ailments (i.e. emotions and behavior)?*

A. Yes, God can heal more than just physical ailments! He has come that you may have abundant life in your spirit, soul, and body.

God desires for you to walk in wholeness and healing in every area of your life.

Q. *How does modern medicine and the healthcare industry fit in with God's ability to heal miraculously?*

A. Pray first, and if the symptoms are serious go to a doctor. It is not a lack of faith to go to a doctor. Once you have a diagnosis, you can target the condition better with prayer. The key is not allowing your diagnosis to define you.

The problem is that after receiving a diagnosis, especially a terminal one, people are tempted to identify themselves by their sickness, and then the fight for healing becomes more challenging. It's one thing to believe God to heal you of a sickness; it's another thing altogether to believe God to change your identity. This is why we need to respond to a doctor's diagnosis correctly. We acknowledge the diagnosis as the situation, but we do not accept it as the final word about our condition—God's Word is eternally the last Word on everything! We do not deny the sickness exists; we deny its right to be in our body.

I fight disease any way I can. God uses doctors, but as our faith is developed we will walk in divine health. There is no condemnation in Jesus! It is easier to develop your faith when you are well by meditating on God's promises so that when symptoms of sickness start to manifest you can resist them from taking root.

Q. *Is it true that forgiveness is part of the healing process?*

A. Yes, forgiveness is a powerful part of the healing process. It has been said, "Unforgiveness is taking the poison you want your enemy to take." Forgiveness is a choice. Being able to trust the person you are forgiving can take time, but we should always live in instant forgiveness.

Q. *What are the largest obstacles to receiving a healing miracle?*

A. The largest obstacles to receiving a healing miracle are unrepentant sin, unforgiveness, and underdeveloped faith. Remember, faith is a gift that every believer receives, but it is also a fruit that must be developed.

Q. *If someone prays over me and I get healed, is the person who prayed or God responsible for the healing?*

A. God, moving through the person who prayed for the healing, gets all the credit!

Q. *How do I answer someone who asks me why God won't heal them?*

A. Jesus paid the price for their healing. They are already healed, and as they develop the fruit of faith and resist the devil he must flee. There is no time in eternity, so the timing of the manifestation of the healing is up to God. The faith part is up to us.

The devil loves to cause sickness and get us to question the goodness of God. Be careful to never get angry with God. Our job is to have an intimate relationship with Him. Through *faith* and *patience* the healing will come.

Q. *Should I be concerned with counterfeit miracles?*

A. The Bible warns about false miracles especially in the last days. The two most important keys to separating the true from the counterfeit in the last days are *holiness* and *Israel.* Those who walk in the gift of healing and are not holy in lifestyle or have an unbiblical view on the Jew and Israel will open themselves to evil spirits. The Spirit of God is called the Holy Spirit. Israel is where the Gospel started, and Israel is where Jesus will return. The promise of Genesis 12:3 is true—God will bless those who bless the Jewish people and curse those who curse them.

A miracle proves the Kingdom of God has come to earth.

Q. *Why does it matter that God continues to perform miracles today?*

A. A miracle proves the Kingdom of God has come to earth. When people see miracles it makes them receptive to hearing the Gospel. This is how Jesus, the apostles, and the first disciples got crowds to hear the Good News. Healing miracles are just as much a tool for evangelism as they are a benefit to those who receive the healing.

Q. *What is one Scripture that I should have at the forefront of my mind when attacked by sickness?*

A. I love Matthew 6:10: "*Your kingdom come. Your will be done on earth as it is in heaven.*" There is *no* sickness in heaven. We are called to force the devil to stop his lying symptoms on earth. We are called to agree with God and His Word, not the devil and his lies. Who will you agree with? We are not to deny the symptoms, but we are to deny their right to stay!

Q. *What if someone does all that you teach and still dies from their sickness?*

A. First of all, we do not know all the facts. Only God knows everything. If they were born again, they are in heaven having the time of their lives. When you get to heaven, you will understand. God sometimes calls people home to heaven because of His knowledge of all things. For instance, Isaiah 57:1 says, "*The righteous perishes, and no man takes it to heart… no one considers that the righteous is taken away from evil.*" Never forget Deuteronomy 29:29: "*The secret things belong to the Lord our God.*"

Chapter 7

YOUR SUPERNATURAL LANGUAGES

And these signs will follow those who believe: In My name they will cast out demons; they will speak with new tongues.

—MARK 16:17

One of the most neglected gifts is the gift of speaking in tongues. I believe the devil has fought the Church relentlessly against this because he is well aware of what it unlocks in believers' lives. This is why I can boldly say that one of the greatest tools I know to help you fulfill your destiny is praying in tongues. When you pray in tongues, you are instantly in the supernatural! Paul says in First

Thessalonians 5:17 for us to "*pray without ceasing.*" This is *impossible* without praying in tongues.

My First Supernatural Testimony of Speaking in Tongues

Before I was even a believer, I would attend prayer meetings with Christians who were trying hard to convince me that Jesus was the Messiah. Even though I was not interested in salvation at that time, there was one thing that intrigued me immensely. The believers said they had a supernatural language that came from God.

After I accepted Jesus as Messiah, I wanted that supernatural language. I went to a meeting where a man prayed for me to be baptized in the Holy Spirit. Then he said, "You're filled with the Holy Spirit, you can now speak in tongues." I'm glad that I didn't know anything. I was like a little child in the Spirit. That's the way you are supposed to be. And I started speaking in a supernatural language by faith. But then, immediately, a little voice in my head said, "You're making that up." So, I stopped. I loved God and I didn't want to make something up.

When you pray in tongues, you are instantly in the supernatural!

One day I was with an Orthodox rabbi who had received Jesus. He introduced me to a woman and said, "Sid, this woman wants prayer." She was pregnant and the doctor said she had a stillborn baby. I was just a brand-new believer and this rabbi was asking me to pray for a dead person to come back to life! I didn't know what to pray, so all of a sudden I started praying in my supernatural language that I doubted was from God. After I finished praying, the woman left and the rabbi asked, "Sid, where did you learn that ancient form of Aramaic?" I didn't know Aramaic. I could barely speak Hebrew (I read Hebrew passages at my Bar Mitzvah). He said, "You prayed that the spirit of the child is with God the Father." There is no way I could have said that apart from the Holy Spirit. After that, I never doubted that my supernatural language was real!

Different Rules for Different Tongues

You need to understand that there are different expressions of tongues. This is very important if you are going to start praying in supernatural languages.

In First Corinthians 14:5 (Greek), Paul says, "I want you *all* to speak in tongues." Everyone who is born again and has received the gift of the Spirit of God has the ability to speak in supernatural languages. Otherwise Paul would not have said, "I want you *all* to speak in tongues." There are different kinds of tongues described in the Bible. For instance, if you are in a congregation, you might speak forth a message in tongues and someone will have an interpretation. This is a prophetic expression of tongues, and not everyone has that gift. It is given as the Holy Spirit wills. But Paul wants *everyone* to speak in a supernatural prayer language.

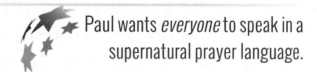 Paul wants *everyone* to speak in a supernatural prayer language.

Just as every sport has different rules, there are different rules for these different types of tongues. People who don't understand this try to combine all the rules for all the different types of tongues, and this is where the confusion comes in. That's sort of like putting football and basketball rules together. It can't work! No wonder people are confused.

In First Corinthians 12:10, Paul says *"to another the working of miracles, to another prophecy, to another discerning of spirits, to another different kinds of tongues."* Let's talk about these different kinds of tongues.

The Gift of Tongues for Witnessing to the Unsaved: Expression of Evangelism

> *And they were all filled with the Holy Spirit and began to speak with other tongues, as the Spirit gave them utterance. ...And when this sound occurred, the multitude came together, and were confused, because everyone heard them speak in his own language. Then they were all amazed and marveled, saying to one another, "Look, are not all these who speak Galileans? And how is it that we hear, each in our own language in which we were born?"* (Acts 2:4,6–8)

First, there is tongues for witnessing to the unsaved. First Corinthians 14:22 says, *"Tongues are for a sign, not to those who believe but to unbelievers."* Here's an example from my own life. Caesar was a Filipino doctor who was not born again and wasn't much interested in spiritual things. His wife, Christina, on the other hand was on fire for the Lord, and she came to a Bible study that I used to lead. At the Bible study, we would pray for Caesar's salvation.

One day, I put my hand on Caesar, and I started speaking in tongues. Caesar looked at me, mystified; then he looked angrily at his wife, and said, "Christina! Did you tell him those words?" And then he thought, *Wait. Christina couldn't have done that because it was in my Filipino dialect; although she's Filipino, her dialect is different from mine. It was exactly in my dialect!* He explained that there are 30 or 40 dialects in the Philippines. I "just happened" to speak in the Filipino language in his dialect. In the book of Acts, it says in the Greek that the people all heard languages in their dialect at Pentecost. I told Caesar in the Filipino language, in his dialect, that he *must* believe in Jesus as the Messiah! Caesar did *amazing* things after he became a believer. I doubt he would have ever gotten saved if he hadn't received that supernatural sign. This operation of tongues is such a wonderful gift for witnessing to non-believers!

The Gift of Tongues in a Congregational Meeting: Expression of the Prophetic

> *There are diversities of gifts, but the same Spirit. There are differences of ministries, but the same Lord. And there are diversities of activities, but it is the same God who works all in all. But the manifestation of the Spirit is given to each one for the profit of all...to another different kinds of tongues, to another the interpretation of tongues* (1 Corinthians 12:4–7,10).

Another use of tongues is in congregational meetings. In First Corinthians 12:28, Paul says, *"And God has appointed these in the church...varieties of tongues."* In other words, there's a special gift of tongues for when there's a group present. Paul goes on to ask, *"Do all speak with tongues? Do all interpret?"* (1 Cor. 12:30). No. Not everyone has the gift of public speaking in tongues. And not everyone has the public gift of interpreting tongues. But Paul is not talking here about tongues as a private prayer language. We need to be careful not to mix up the rules.

The Gift of Tongues as a Private Prayer Language: Available to All Believers

> *Now I wish that you might all speak in [unknown] tongues* (1 Corinthians 14:5 AMPC).

First Corinthians 14:5 tells us how a spirit-filled meeting in the first Church operated. I believe this was the secret behind the power of the first Jewish believers in the Messiah. Acts 6:4 says, *"We will give ourselves continually to prayer and to the ministry of the word."* You may be familiar with that wording, but this is what it says in the Greek: "We will give ourselves continually to ['the'] prayer." What was *the* prayer? Paul gives us a clue. He said in First Corinthians 14:18, *"I thank my God I speak with tongues more than you all."* "I speak"—the man who wrote most of the New Testament thought it was important to speak in tongues more than anyone else.

Paul says, *"I will pray with the Spirit, and I will also pray with the understanding. I will sing with the spirit, and I will also sing with the understanding"* (1 Cor. 14:15). And then in verse 26 he says, *"How is it then, brethren? Whenever you come together, each of you has a psalm, has a teaching, has a tongue, has a revelation, has an interpretation. Let all things be done for edification."*

Another type of tongues is your personal prayer language. This isn't public; this is your prayer to God. In First Corinthians 14:2 Paul says, *"For he who speaks in a tongue does not speak to men but to God."* Every time you pray in your supernatural language, you are speaking to God! Do you realize how holy and wonderful this is?

There are three ways to pray in your supernatural language. The most powerful way is to pray in tongues out loud. Why out loud? Because there is extra power in the spoken word. But sometimes you are in a situation where you can't, especially when you are with nonbelievers. In those situations you can pray in tongues under your breath without moving your lips. The third way is to think the language to yourself just as you think your known language to yourself. All three ways are very powerful!

The most anointed believers I know pray out loud in supernatural languages for hours every day. They move in major miracles, and you can feel the tangible presence of God when you are around them. But now you can be like Paul. Paul said in First Corinthians 14:18, *"I speak with tongues more than you all."* Begin to pray in supernatural languages all the time—without ceasing!

 There is extra power in the spoken word.

Praying in Tongues: Prophesying Your Future

Do you realize when you pray in tongues you are prophesying your future? When you speak into the atmosphere what God has for your future, you are speaking it in perfect faith!

If I could go back to the days when I first started praying in tongues and eavesdrop with revelation on what I was saying, I believe I was prophesying that one day we would have a worldwide television ministry. Lately, I know I've been prophesying what is yet going to happen in my ministry. Everything we have done to date is in preparation for what is about ready to unfold! But it never would have happened if I hadn't prayed perfect prayers with perfect faith in those early years. It's not too late for you! You will not miss your destiny! Start praying an hour a day in supernatural languages.

When you pray in tongues, you are bypassing your mind and praying from your spirit. Your mind doesn't know what you are doing, so it can't argue with you. It's like saying, "Mind, be quiet. I'm putting my spirit in charge." When you pray in that supernatural language, there is no doubt. None whatsoever. You're praying with perfect faith. In the natural, you only see the tip of the iceberg when you pray for someone using intelligible languages. You're praying for that little bit of the iceberg, but the real action is in the invisible world. When you pray in tongues, you are praying with all knowledge and wisdom, past, present, and future.

Benefits of Praying in Supernatural Languages

What if the Holy Spirit knew everything that would make things right? You could pray perfect prayers by the Holy Spirit in perfect faith. Do you realize what a weapon that is? Now you are beginning to understand why the enemy doesn't want you to pray in tongues. Could it be that this is why there has been such a strategic attack against speaking in tongues over the centuries? It has always been controversial—but why? It's clearly spelled out in Scripture. Some of the most notable and respected theologians of our current day recognize the continuation of tongues as both a prophetic expression and private prayer language—Craig Keener, Wayne Grudem, and Gordon Fee, to name a free. The devil attacks what he is afraid of and he will do whatever he can to create a civil war among believers, arguing over something that is not only clearly presented in the Bible but releases enormous supernatural power.

Even in some churches where they believe in tongues, they have demoted it to a back room or even pushed it out of the Church completely. Why? It drives the devil crazy!

By the time I finish teaching you, some of you are not going to be able to stop praying in tongues. It's going to break out within you. So I encourage you, read the following pages with expectation. Get hungry for more of God.

> *Likewise the Spirit also helps in our weaknesses. For we do not know what we should pray for as we ought, but the Spirit Himself makes intercession for us with groanings which cannot be uttered. Now He who searches the hearts knows what the mind of the Spirit is, because He makes intercession for the saints according to the will of God. And we know that all things work together for*

good to those who love God, to those who are the called according to His purpose (Romans 8:26-28).

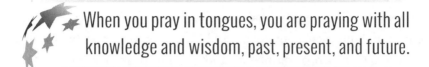 When you pray in tongues, you are praying with all knowledge and wisdom, past, present, and future.

How would you like *all* things to work together for good in your life? God promises that to us. We quote His promise from Romans 8:28, but most don't take into account the prior verses. So what causes all things to work together for good in your life? Praying in supernatural languages.

There are several benefits of speaking in tongues.

1. Praying Perfect Prayers with Perfect Faith

Romans 8:26 says, *"Likewise the Spirit also helps in our weaknesses."* The word for "weakness" in the Greek means "sickness." Do you realize that when you are praying in supernatural languages you are praying perfect prayers in the areas of your life that have to be rectified to get rid of the sickness that has its ugly hook in you? I'd have been praying in tongues day and night if I had understood this.

Then, in verse 27 Paul writes, *"Now He who searches the hearts knows what the mind of the Spirit is, because He makes intercession for the saints according to the will of God."* Every prayer you pray in tongues is according to the will of God who knows *everything*. We know *nothing* compared to the One who knows *everything* and we are able to pray the same way God would be praying for someone's problem! Can you see how important this is?

Paul goes on to say in verse 28, *"And we know that all things work together for good to those who love God, to those who are the called according to His purpose."* Do you want everything to "work together for good" in your life? Pray perfect prayers! Pray through the power of the One who knows *everything*. There is *never* a time you pray in tongues that something supernaturally good is not happening! You should be excited every time you pray in tongues. You should pray in tongues like Paul—more than any person! You will solve your emotional problems, physical problems, financial problems, marital problems, people problems, and destiny problems all by praying in tongues.

There is *never* a time you pray in tongues that something supernaturally good is not happening!

2. Building Up Your Spirit Man

Jude 1:20 tells you *why* you should speak in tongues: *"But you, beloved, building yourself up on your most holy faith, praying in the Holy Spirit."* In other words, you are building up your spirit man— your spirit is actually growing!

A few years ago, I started tripping and falling down. I thought, "I walk a half hour a day. Why am I falling?" And someone said to me, "Walking doesn't build muscles." So I went to a gym and started lifting weights. I had a personal trainer who helped me, and if I hadn't had that personal trainer I would not have gotten the firm foundation that I have today. And guess what? I don't fall anymore! Well, it's the same thing in the spirit realm. As a new believer, I prayed in tongues an hour a day. But you know how it is—over time, I prayed less and less. Now, I'm back with a vengeance and I don't want a day to go by that I don't pray for one hour in tongues. And I don't want a day to go by that you don't pray for one hour in tongues! Now, my goal is to pray in tongues *all* the time!

There is no limit to how much God wants to use you in these last days. *"Eye has not seen, nor ear heard"* what God has in store for you (1 Cor. 2:9). But it will not happen unless you build up your spirit man, and that's what happens when you pray in tongues. It says you *edify yourself* (see 1 Cor. 14:4). *Edify* in Greek is a word that means "you charge up your battery." You charge up your spiritual battery by meditating on the Word of God and praying in supernatural languages.

3. *Praising God All the Time*

How would you like to praise God all the time? The truth is you don't have the ability to praise God 24/7 in English. But listen to what Paul says in First Corinthians 14:17: *"For you indeed give thanks well"* when you are praying in tongues. Do you want to give thanks well? Pray and sing in supernatural languages.

> The more you pray in supernatural languages, the more His love is going to pour out on everyone you meet.

4. *Becoming God-Inside Conscious*

When you pray in tongues, you become "God-inside" conscious. In other words, you become increasingly aware of the Holy Spirit who lives inside of you. Many years ago, I read *The Practice of the Presence of God* by Brother Lawrence. When you are praying from your spirit, do you realize that you are praying God's words? You are practicing the presence of God. When I'm praying in supernatural languages I am conscious of God every moment because the prayer is coming from my spirit, not from my mind. This kind of prayer literally comes out of the place within me where God the Holy Spirit resides.

Brother Lawrence was a monk who performed menial tasks like washing dishes. Yet the most important people of the land would seek him out because there was such an explosion of the love of God pouring out of him. This man had no money and no education. But he was conscious of God.

Everyone wants to believe that God is personal. Everyone wants to know this God. The more you pray in supernatural languages, the more His love is going to pour out on everyone you meet. Let's suppose your spouse is not a believer and asks you to attend a cocktail party. You go because you love your spouse. You don't preach to anyone because your spouse has asked you not to. But you won't have to. Because you are praying in tongues, God's love will pour out of you and people will be drawn to you.

5. Removing the Blockages to Fulfilling Your Destiny

Your power in the spirit is going to be increased as you pray in tongues. Spiritual gifts will be released. Blockages in your life that are stopping you from fulfilling your destiny will be eliminated. You're going to get rid of hurts. Sometimes when I pray in tongues, I'll think about someone who hurt me. It could have been an event from decades ago, something I don't even think about anymore. And while I'm praying in tongues, I'm able to forgive that person. It's the most wonderful gift! You'll start having revelation of the Word of God like you've never had in your life as you pray in tongues.

6. Supernatural Protection

Several years ago, I interviewed a woman who prayed in tongues for an hour before she went to the grocery store. As she got out of her car, a man pulled a gun on her and forced her to drive to a wooded area. What she didn't know was this man was wanted by the police for having raped and murdered 30 women who looked similar to her. Because she prayed in tongues for an hour, she had supernatural protection. This man not only did not rape or murder her, but he surrendered to the police and received Jesus.

7. Supernatural Revelation

Do you want more revelation from God? You're going to be sensitive to God's voice when you pray in your supernatural language. You're going to walk in His tangible presence. You're going to have supernatural favor and peace.

Even the chemistry of your brain is going to change. Dr. Carl Peterson, MD—a brain specialist—found out through research and testing that when we pray from our spirit, there is activity that begins to take place in our brain. As we engage in our heavenly language, the brain releases chemical secretions that are directed into our immune system, giving it a boost. Praying in tongues even promotes healing within our bodies.

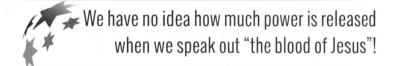 We have no idea how much power is released when we speak out "the blood of Jesus"!

Ready, Set, Pray in Supernatural Languages!

Acts 2:4 says, *"And they were all filled with the Holy Spirit and began to speak with other tongues."* Who did the speaking? The people did. If you don't open your mouth and make a sound, no one else will. If you don't, it's like saying, "I'm waiting for God to take over my tongue." This is perhaps one of the biggest misconceptions when it comes to praying in tongues; we are mistakenly waiting for God to supernaturally take over our mouth and do the speaking for us.

Peter walked on water. Do you know why? Jesus was walking on the water and Peter thought, "That's pretty cool. Can I walk on water like that?" Jesus said, "Come," and Peter responded, "If You'll move my legs for me I'll come to You"—right? No. He didn't say that. He stood up. He knew how to walk. He'd been doing it his whole life. He swung his foot over the side of the boat and stepped out on the water. Who did the walking? Peter.

Who does the talking when we are speaking in tongues? We do. Peter did his part and your part is to speak from your spirit. You might be thinking, "I don't know what to say." Perfect! It's called *unknown* tongues. "But what if it's not from God?" What if it *is* from God? My Bible says that if a child asks for bread, his father is not going to give him a stone (see Matt. 7:9). How much more will our heavenly Father give the Holy Spirit to those who ask in the name of Jesus? If your heart is set to receive this wonderful gift from the Holy Spirit, I can assure you, you will not receive something evil or demonic. Let the first words you speak before tongues come out be, "the blood of Jesus." Repeat that about 20 times. This will clear out the atmosphere of the demonic. No counterfeit could dare show up! We have no idea how much power is released when we speak out "the blood of Jesus"!

If you have never prayed in supernatural languages and you would like to, I want you to say this prayer and mean it with all your heart:

> *Dear God, I'm a sinner. Against You and You alone have I sinned and I'm so sorry. I believe that Jesus died in my place, and by His blood You remember my sins no more. Now that I am clean, I ask Jesus to be my Lord. Lord Jesus, come and live inside of me, and in Jesus' name I ask You to fill me from the top of my head to the bottom of my toes with Your Holy Spirit and with Your power. Amen.*

Now, be like Peter in the Bible. Get out of the boat! Speak by faith as quickly as you can. Say out loud, "In Jesus' Name, take the words that come out of my mouth as worship unto You."

Become like a little child. It would be simple if you were a child. So start speaking as if you were five years old and wanted to please your father.

Start speaking, even if you have to start with just a few syllables. Now begin to increase the speed so that you are speaking as fast as you can.

Some of you are at a stalemate. This is Sid, your coach, telling you if you don't do the speaking, no one else will do it for you! If you don't know what to say, that's perfect. It's coming from your spirit and *not* your brain. You will not hear it until *you* speak it out loud.

After a few minutes of speaking, I want you to stop. This is the only gift of the Spirit that you control. You can start and stop when you are praying in English and you can start and stop praying when it's from your spirit.

In First Corinthians 14:15, Paul says that you can sing in your spirit and you can sing in your understanding. You can pray in the spirit and you can pray in your understanding. Oral Roberts taught that you can develop a rhythm. You're praying in tongues; then you're praying with your understanding. And if you do this long enough, you will begin to interpret your own tongues. You'll be getting direction from the Spirit.

Years ago, I attended a Kenneth E. Hagin meeting, and he called me out along with a friend of mine and prophesied over me. By the way, Kenneth is in heaven now, but that prophecy is coming true. Then he prophesied over my friend who is also a Jewish believer and is also involved in ministry worldwide. He prophesied over my friend in tongues because he said it's no one's business. When you are praying in tongues, unless God gives you the interpretation, the devil doesn't have a clue what's being said. He can't sabotage you. You are praying perfect prayers in perfect faith with no satanic resistance. Now you understand why the devil doesn't want you to pray for hours in tongues!

After I became a believer and realized I really was speaking in a supernatural language, I used to go out to a meeting of Catholic Charismatics at Georgetown University in Washington, D.C. At these meetings, most of the people didn't know each other. But when we all came together and were praying and singing in different languages it was like a great choir singing in harmony. By the way, did you know there are tongues of angels? Paul talks about that in the love chapter. He writes, *"Though I speak with the tongues of men and of angels"* (1 Cor. 13:1). Do you realize you are releasing the angels with no resistance from the enemy when you are praying in tongues? If people only understood all that was available to them through this wonderful gift!

> When you are praying in tongues, unless God gives you the interpretation, the devil doesn't have a clue what's being said. He can't sabotage you. You are praying perfect prayers in perfect faith with no satanic resistance.

Always remember, according to the Word of God, you are not speaking to man when you are praying in a supernatural language—you are speaking to God. And as you pray in tongues, every gift of the Spirit is going to be activated in your life.

As we move into the third section of this book, I want to give you the key that will unlock the greatest release of the supernatural in the Church and in your life. This is something that many don't talk about, and yet I believe it's why we are not experiencing the measure of miracle-working power that God desires to unleash into the world.

Part Three

YOUR SUPERNATURAL ASSIGNMENT

When you learn how to use the supernatural tools you've been given, you will discover how those tools are directly linked to you fulfilling your destiny in God.

For years, people have been talking and prophesying about the "great move of God" that will impact the entire world. Are we waiting on God, or is God waiting on us? I know God is waiting on us!

Chapter 8

YOUR GREATEST MIRACLE

If you heed the word I am about to share, it will change your life dramatically. You will walk in the favor and power of God no matter what happens on planet earth. If you do not heed this word, you will walk in curses.

When the Messiah came to earth over 2,000 years ago, things were simpler than today. The world was divided into two people groups. There were Jewish people who lived in the land of Israel, and there were Gentiles. The word *Gentile* means "nations." There is a call by God for people who are from the Gentile nations that is different from the call by God for people who are part of Israel.

Let me explain this from Scripture. Romans 11:11 says, "*to provoke them* [the Jewish people] *to jealousy, salvation is come to the Gentiles.*" The call of the Gentile is to provoke the Jew to jealousy. This means that Gentiles have something that we Jewish people want, and it's time to show it. If not now, when?

The call of the Jew is very different. John 4:22 says, *"salvation is of the Jews."* A Gentile who believes in Jesus owes a debt of gratitude to the Jewish people because some Jewish person was faithful to share the good news with Gentiles. If the Gentiles do their job and reach the Jews and if the Jewish people do their job and reach the Gentiles, guess what you've got? The whole world!

Israel Is the Dividing Line

It's also important to understand that God judges the nations based on their treatment of Israel. In the last days, this judgment is increasing with intensity. God will punish Israel for sin, but God uses Israel to punish the nations for sin.

Genesis 12:3 says, *"I [God] will bless those who bless you [that's the Jewish people] and curse those who treat you with contempt. All the families on earth will be blessed through you"* (NLT). And the reverse is also true—*all the families of the earth if they come against you will be cursed.*

This principle is still in full force and effect today. For example, many of the worst economic disasters in the history of America (such as Hurricane Katrina) have occurred within days or hours of the United States coming against Israel.[1]

Obadiah 1:15 says, *"The day is near when I, the Lord, will judge all godless nations! As you have done to Israel, so it will be done to you. All your evil deeds will fall back on your own heads"* (NLT).

Let me give you the same principle from the New Testament. In Matthew 25:40, Jesus says the goat nations and sheep nations will be separated on one issue: *"And the King will answer and say to them, 'Assuredly, I say to you, inasmuch as you did it to one of the least of these My brethren,* [Jesus says] *you did it to Me.'"* What's the difference between a goat and a sheep? A goat has a mind of its own and the sheep follows the shepherd. "As you have done to one of the least of these *My brethren.*" The word for "brethren" in the Greek means "from the womb." Jesus is talking about how each nation has treated His physical brethren, the Jewish people.

In recent years, many major universities, church pension funds, and big corporations have been disinvesting rather than investing in Israel. They are trying to force Israel to give land to the Palestinians that God has given to the Jewish people (see Ps. 105:8–11).

Divesting from Israel is plain *meshuga* (Hebrew for crazy)! This is a dangerous time for the anti-Semites of the world—they are going against God and bringing themselves under judgment.

On the other hand, those who obey God regarding Israel and the Jewish people are blessed. Remember when Pharaoh told the midwives in Egypt to kill all the male babies at birth? They refused to curse Israel, and what did God do? Exodus 1:20-21 says, "*So God was good to the midwives, and the Israelites continued to multiply, growing more and more powerful. And because the midwives feared God, he gave them families of their own*" (NLT).

I recently read where Liberty University has invested $5 million in Israeli stocks. No wonder that university is blessed!

I believe the dividing line between the true Body of believers and the counterfeit in these last days will be on this single issue. If you don't understand the Jew and Israel from God's perspective, then you will drift into further heresy. But if you do understand, watch the favor of God flow in your life. This is the secret to seeing the fullness of God's power released on the earth.

First the Natural, Then the Spiritual

A key to understanding the move of God's Spirit is found in First Corinthians 15:46, in which God says first comes the natural and then the spiritual. Watch what God does in the natural. It always has a repercussion in the spiritual. Let me give you some examples.

In 1897, the first Zionist Congress was convened. A Zionist believes the Jewish people are entitled to the physical land of Israel, unconditionally, forever. The first Zionist was God! Shortly after this move toward reestablishing a Jewish homeland came the Azusa Street and the Pentecostal revivals.

In 1948, Israel became a nation. Do you know what else happened? Men and women were touched by the Spirit of God and raised up to hold tent meetings all over America including people like Oral Roberts, T.L. Osborn, and Kenneth Hagin.

In 1967, Jerusalem came back into Jewish possession. What did that trigger in the spiritual? Nothing short of the Charismatic revival.

What will bring completeness to Jerusalem?
Jew and Gentile being one in the Messiah.

One New Man

Isaiah 43:19 says, *"For I am about to do something new. See, I have already begun. Do you not see it?"* (NLT). What has God begun? The One New Man. In John 17:21, Jesus prays that *"they all may be one."* Some people say "they" is different religious groups like Catholics and Baptists. But when Jesus prayed this prayer, they didn't exist. There were only two people groups—Jews and Gentiles. What happens when the two come together? The world will believe. Somehow, there is a catalyst in the Spirit when these two people groups unite. Their spiritual DNA merges. What happens then? In John 17:22 Jesus says, *"The glory which You gave Me I have given them."* Do you want to see that same glory on you?

In Ephesians 2:14 and 22, Paul writes, *"For He Himself is our peace, who has made both* [Jew and Gentile] *one, and has broken down the middle wall of separation* [there was a separation between Jews and Gentiles]...*in whom you are also being built together for a dwelling place of God in the spirit."* And in verse 15 Paul says, *"so as to create in Himself one new man from the two, thus making peace."* The Hebrew word for "peace" is *shalom*, which means "completeness." When Jew and Gentile come together in the Messiah, we are going to make a complete dwelling place for God by His Spirit.

Now you can understand God's promise in Psalm 122:6 where He says, *"Pray for the peace of Jerusalem: 'May they prosper who love you.'"* Jerusalem is the only city in all of Scripture that God commands us to pray for with a special blessing. We have just learned that peace means completeness. What will bring completeness to Jerusalem? Jew and Gentile being one in the Messiah. When God says *"May they prosper,"* the Hebrew word for "prosper" means to have heart peace. How would you like to have heart peace? God said if you will pray for the completeness of Jerusalem by Jew and Gentile becoming one, you are going to have heart peace. That's His promise to you.

Ezekiel 47:9 describes the river of God: *"Wherever the double river shall go, every living creature...shall live"* (AMPC). What's the double river? Jew and Gentile, one in Messiah Yeshua. Wherever that double river goes, it brings the life of God.

Romans 11:15 says, *"If their* [the Jewish people's] *being cast away is the reconciling of the world, what will their acceptance be but life from the dead?"* I believe we are on the cutting edge of the greatest move of God's Spirit to cause Jewish people to come to know Him. As they come together with the Gentile Church, they will form the One New Man, releasing the greatest demonstration of miracles the world has ever seen. These miracles will include people being raised from the dead and creative miracles such as limbs being restored. Are you ready to see that? Jesus said that you are going to do the same works that He has done and even greater. This is the greater. Are you ready? I'm ready!

When you go to the Jew first, you open a door of blessing.

The Mystery Law of Evangelism

Many Bible believers know the spiritual laws about healing. Many also know the spiritual laws of prosperity. Both of these are valid and important. But you can't take your money to heaven. And you won't need healing in heaven. The only thing you take to heaven is souls! This is why Proverbs 11:30 says, *"he who wins souls is wise."*

I have found that most believers do not know that there is also a Law of Evangelism. The key is to go "to the Jew first." When **God** wanted to reach the world, He went first to the Jew, Abram, who was renamed Abraham. We know God loved all people. So why did He go to the Jew first?

When **Jesus** wanted to reach the world, He went to the Jew first. Matthew 15:24 says, *"But He [Jesus] answered and said, 'I was not sent except to the lost sheep of the house of Israel.'"* We know Jesus loved all people. So why did He go to the Jew first?

When **Paul**, the apostle to the Gentiles, wanted to reach the Gentiles, he went to the Jew first. In Romans 1:16, Paul writes, *"For I am not ashamed of the gospel of Messiah, for it is the power of God to salvation for everyone who believes, for the Jew first and also for the Greek."*

We know Paul was called to the Gentiles. So why did he go to the Jew first? He certainly received more than his fair share of persecution from unsaved Jewish people. Acts 18:6 states, *"But when they opposed* [Paul] *and blasphemed, he shook his garments and said to them, 'Your blood be upon your own heads; I am clean. From now on I will go to the Gentiles.'"* Yet even after this statement of utter exasperation, the next two verses show Paul *still* went to the Jew first: *"And* [Paul] *departed from there and entered the house of a certain man named Justus, one who worshiped God, whose house was next door to the synagogue. Then Crispus, the ruler of the synagogue, believed on the Lord with all his household"* (Acts 18:7-8).

God, Jesus, and Paul knew that when you go to the Jew first you reach more Gentiles than if you go to the Gentile first. Why? When you go to the Jew first, you open a door of blessing based on Genesis 12:3. In this Scripture, God promises to bless those who bless the Jewish people. *What is the greatest way to bless the Jewish people?* Tell them about the Good News of Jesus. When you do this, you are planting a seed that will result in a harvest of Gentile souls. You are also sowing into the salvation of your own family.

If I create evangelistic literature to reach Gentiles, I will reach very few Jewish people. But when I design evangelistic materials to reach Jewish people, I will reach multitudes of Gentiles as well!

The Law of Evangelism makes no sense to our natural minds. But it makes a lot of sense to God.

The greatest revival the world will ever see is described in Amos 9:11 and 13. This is what God says: *"On that day* [the last days] *I will raise up the tabernacle of David."* In the Hebrew the word *tabernacle* means "family" or "house." Who is the family of David? The Jewish people. In the last days, God will raise up the Jewish people to be mighty warriors, mighty evangelists. Then God describes the coming revival in Amos 9:13. He says there will be so much fruit on the vine that when the time comes to till the ground for the next year's planting, we won't have picked all the fruit from the last year's harvest. The world has never seen a revival like this. The world needs a revival like this! When is it going to happen? When the family of David (Jewish people) is restored to God.

Even the return of Jesus is contingent on Jewish people coming to the Lord. Jesus said to the Jewish people in Matthew 23:39, "you shall see Me no more" till you say *Baruch Ha'ba Ba Shem Adonai*—blessed is He who comes in the Name of the Lord. He is saying, "I'm not going to return until you recognize Me."

I Wish I Were Jewish!

Don't Jewish people have a special covenant with God? Of course we do, and the gifts and calling of God are without repentance. However, the old covenant is contingent on Leviticus 17:11 which says, "*the life of the flesh is in the blood, and I have given it to you upon the altar to make atonement for your souls; for it is the blood that makes atonement for the soul.*" Without the shedding of blood there is no forgiveness of sin. What about just having animal sacrifices to atone for sin? First of all, according to Leviticus 1:3, the sacrifice has to be in the Temple. Have you looked lately? There is no Temple in Jerusalem. And Acts 4:12 clinches it: "*Nor is there salvation in any other, for there is no other name under heaven given among men in which we must be saved* [but the name of Jesus]."

Everyone has heard that the Jewish people are the chosen people, but what are we chosen for? Isaiah 43:10 says, "*You are my witnesses.*" Do you know what the word *Jew* comes from? The Hebrew word *Yehuda,* which means a praiser of God. Jewish people are called to be witnesses, praisers of God, and super end-time evangelists.

Zechariah 8:23 says, "*Thus says the Lord of hosts: 'In those days ten men from every language of the nations* [that's the Gentiles] *shall grasp the sleeve* [the fringes] *of a Jewish man, saying, "Let us go with you, for we have heard that God is with you.""*

A lot of people are interested in knowing what great thing the Jewish people did in order to be so blessed by God. Here's the answer: *"The Lord did not set His love on you nor choose you because you were more in number than any other people, for you were the least of all peoples; but because the Lord loves you, and because He would keep the oath which He swore to your fathers"* (Deut. 7:7-8). What was the oath? The oath was involving the land of Israel and the Messiah. Who were the fathers? Abraham, Isaac, and Jacob.

Now about this time many from a non-Jewish background begin thinking, "I wish I were Jewish." Some might even join a Messianic synagogue and act more Jewish than the Jewish people in that synagogue. If that thought has crossed your mind, I've got an amazing word for you.

 If you do not know what hurts me, how can you say you love me?

Do you remember the story of the prodigal son? I see the father as a type of God the Father. The younger brother is a type of the Jewish believer who threw away his inheritance. And the older brother represents the Gentile Christian who has worked in the Father's vineyard for the last 2,000 years. When the prodigal returns home after squandering his inheritance, his father runs to him and hugs him. He gives him his robe. He throws a lavish party with music, singing, and dancing. The older brother has been working in the field, and when he finally gets back home he is immediately envious of all the fuss over the younger brother's return. The father sees the older brother sulking and says to him, *"Son, you are always with me, and all that I have is yours"* (Luke 15:31).

There is no room for jealousy. I'll tell you what there is room for. There is room for you to reach your Jewish friend with the Gospel and walk arm and arm with him to form a full dwelling place of God on earth and do the same works as Jesus and even greater!

"Christian" Anti-Semitism?

There's an old Hassidic story about a Talmudic student who goes to his rabbi and says, "Oh master, I love you."

The rabbi responds with a question: "Tell me. Do you know what hurts me?"

The young man is taken aback. He wonders, "Why do you ask me such a confusing question when I've just told you that I love you?"

The rabbi shakes his head. "Because if you do not know what hurts me, how can you say you love me?"

Why do most Jewish people not believe in Jesus? One major reason is the tragic history of "Christian" anti-Semitism. These two words should never even go together. Let me share with you facts about some of the early Church fathers that few Bible students know.[2]

- **Eusebius** alleged that Jews engaged in ceremonial killing of Christian children each year at Purim.

- **St. Hillary of Poitiers** said that the Jews were a perverse people, forever accursed by God.

- **St. John Chrysostom** said that "there could never be expiation [atonement] for the Jews" and that "God had always hated them." He said it was incumbent upon all Christians to hate the Jews. They were "assassins of Christ and worshippers of the devil." Chrysostom stated, "The synagogue is worse than a brothel. It is the temple of demons."[3]

- **St. Augustine** said the true image of the Jew was Judas Iscariot—forever guilty. For their own good and for the good of society, Jews must be relegated to the position of slaves. Augustine believed that because of their sin against the Messiah the Jews rightly deserved death.[4]

- In AD 1099, **the Crusaders** herded the Jews into the great synagogue in Jerusalem. With the Jews inside and the doors locked, they set the building ablaze and marched around singing "Christ We Adore Thee" as the Jews were screaming and dying.

- **Martin Luther** said the Jews were ritual murderers and poisoners of wells. He called for all synagogues to be destroyed. The *Encyclopedia Judaica* commented on Luther: "Short of the Auschwitz oven and concentration camps the whole Nazi Holocaust is pre-outlined here."[5] Indeed, Adolph Hitler wrote in his book, *Mein Kampf,* "I believe I'm acting in accordance with the mighty Creator by defending myself against the Jew. I am fighting for the work of the Lord."[6]

Several years ago, I interviewed a holocaust survivor named Rose Price. Rose saw hundreds of her family members murdered in the concentration camps. As a child she was sent to one of the worst camps. On the archway over the entrance to the camp it said, "We kill you because you killed our God, Jesus Christ." Rose survived, but she had such a hatred in her heart toward Christianity that she wanted to burn churches. One day after she had married and moved to America, her teenage daughter came home and announced she believed in Jesus. To Rose, it was as if her daughter had said, "I just married Adolph Hitler." Then a great miracle happened. Rose became a Messianic Jew, a believer in Jesus as her Messiah. Only God could do this.

Jesus said in John 13:35, *"By this all will know that you are My disciples, if you have love."* So don't tell me how big your cross is, show me you are a disciple of Jesus by your love. Many Christians died as martyrs to save Jews during the Holocaust. There is even a park in Israel to honor them, a garden of the righteous martyrs, and things are changing. Christians are beginning to understand that they owe a debt of gratitude to the Jewish people because Jesus the Messiah is Jewish.

Today, there is a new, more subtle anti-Semitism. People say, "I'm not against the Jew; I'm just against Zionism." Zionism believes that the Jews are entitled to the land of Israel unconditionally forever. Who owns the land of Israel? This is what God says in Joel 3:2: *"I will also gather all nations...and I will enter into judgment with them there on account of My people, My heritage Israel, whom they have scattered among the nations; they have also divided up My land."* So, Israel is not owned by the Jews. Israel is not owned by the Arabs. Israel is owned by God. If you own something, you have the right to lease it. The terms of the lease are found in Psalm 105:8–11 where God says He gives the land to the Jewish people. For how long? He says it in three different ways. He says *"forever."* That's a pretty long time. He also says *"everlasting."* If you can't envision forever or everlasting, He says it a third way—*"for a thousand generations."* That is an airtight lease.

> Don't tell me how big your cross is, show me you are a disciple of Jesus by your love.

One of the Greatest Miracles in the Bible

To understand the heart of the Jew you must understand that God promised to preserve the Jewish people:

> *Thus says the Lord, who gives the sun for a light by day, the ordinances of the moon and the stars for a light by night, who disturbs the sea, and its waves roar (the Lord of hosts is His name): "If those ordinances depart from before Me, says the Lord, then the seed of Israel shall also cease from being a nation before Me forever"* (Jeremiah 31:35-36).

In other words, God promised that as long as there was an earth there would be Jewish people as a distinct race. This is one of the greatest miracles in the Bible.

Imagine a people that lose their country and are scattered to the four corners of the earth. And for 2,000 years they are murdered and persecuted in every country in which they settle—just for being Jews. You would think that by now every Jew would have either assimilated into another religion just to survive or been murdered.

 Gentile believers are joint heirs of the promises of Abraham, but the Church has not replaced Israel.

How did God cause the Jews to survive as a distinct people? God put an *instinct* in the heart of every Jew that says, "I was born a Jew and I will die a Jew." Christians often assume that a Jew who never goes to the synagogue or who considers himself secular or even an atheist is not interested in being Jewish. Untrue! So if you tell a nominal Jew that in order to become a Christian he needs to *stop being Jewish* you are going against a God-given *instinct.* The rabbis say you cannot be Jewish and believe in Jesus. And many in the Church say you cannot be Jewish and believe in Jesus. The result is that we Jews feel we can believe in anything *except* Jesus.

You don't stop being Jewish when you become a follower of the Jewish Messiah any more than you stop being a male or a female (see Gal. 3:28). Even Paul, *after* accepting Jesus, said in Acts 21:39, *"I am a Jew,"* not "I *was* a Jew"! I, Sid Roth, am a Jew, and I will die a Jew.

Common Misconceptions

There are so many misconceptions among Christians about the Jewish people. One major erroneous teaching is called *replacement theology.* What that basically means is that **the Church has replaced Israel in God's plan.** The Church inherits all the promises in the Bible that are meant for Israel and Israel gets all the curses. It's hard for me to believe that someone can read the Bible and come to that conclusion. For instance, if you read Romans 9, 10, and 11, it's clear that God has not given up on Israel. But assume for a moment that the Church has replaced Israel. Let me substitute the word *Church* for *Israel* in just one sentence from Romans 11:28 "Concerning the Gospel, the *Church* is an enemy." Does that make any sense? No! It can't be the Church. It has to be Israel. Gentile believers are joint heirs of the promises of Abraham, but the Church has not replaced Israel.

A second misconception is that **the Jews killed the Messiah.** Acts 4:27 tells us the truth about who killed Jesus: *"For truly against Your holy Servant Jesus, whom You anointed, both Herod and Pontius Pilate, with the Gentiles and the people of Israel, were gathered together."* So who killed Jesus? Herod, Pontius Pilate, the Jews, the Gentiles—the whole world. He wasn't killed; He laid down His life.

He could have had 10,000 angels to defend Him. He died as the innocent Lamb who takes away the sins of the world.

A third misconception is that **Jewish people know the Old Testament better than Christians**. We Jewish people know the same stories that you know from Sunday school. That's all. But you know them better than we do. The average Christian who has been in church all his life knows the Old Testament better than 99 percent of the Jewish people. In sharing with a Jewish person, you might ask them to read Isaiah 53 because it contains so many prophecies about Jesus, but many don't even know who Isaiah is.

A fourth misconception is that **Jewish people are not interested in Jesus or spiritual things**. Did you know that in the New Age the majority of the leaders are Jewish? Why? Romans 10:2 says about the Jewish people that we "*have a zeal for God, but not according to knowledge*." First Corinthians 1:22 tells us how to reach a Jew. The Jew requires a sign! You are being mentored to move in the supernatural of God to reach the Jew to ultimately reach the world. It's really simple.

A fifth misconception is that the **Jewish people are under a curse and cannot be saved until after the Rapture**. Actually, we Jewish people are under a curse of spiritual blindness, but we're told in Scripture when it will be lifted. Romans 11:25 says this "*blindness in part* [in part meaning there are still some Jewish people who believe in Jesus] *has happened to Israel until the fullness of the Gentiles has come in*." So when the fullness of the Gentiles comes in, then the blindness will be removed from the eyes of the Jewish people. Luke 21:24 tells us when the fullness will come in: "*And they* [the Jewish people] *will fall by the edge of the sword, and be led away captive into all nations. And Jerusalem will be trampled by the Gentiles until the times of the Gentiles be fulfilled*." So when is this going to be? When Jerusalem is in Jewish possession. When did that happen? Israel regained control of Jerusalem in 1967.

> It is imperative to reach the Jewish people with the Gospel. This is the key to seeing the greatest release of miracles, signs, and wonders the world has ever seen.

We're at the fullness of the Gentile age. One of the definitions of the Greek word for fullness is "mature." When the Gentile Christians get mature in the Word of God and move in signs and wonders, the spiritual scales will be blasted away and you will see multitudes of Jewish people coming to the Lord.

Four Ways to Be Normal

Now that you understand *why* it is imperative to reach the Jewish people with the Gospel, you need to learn *how* to reach them. This is the key to seeing the greatest release of miracles, signs, and wonders the world has ever seen. The next chapter will go into more detail, but here is a brief summary of four ways to share the Good News with the Jewish person God will have cross your path.

1. **By operating in what some of the early Church fathers did not—in the God kind of love.** It's different than natural love. The God kind of love is explained in First Corinthians 13:4-8. You can't do it without God, but you *can* do it *with* God.

2. **By moving in the glory of God.** This is a description of the glory of God from Isaiah 60:1-2 (AMPC):

   Arise…! Shine (be radiant with the glory of the Lord), for your light has come, and the glory of the Lord has risen upon you! For behold, darkness shall cover the earth, and dense darkness [all] peoples [a thick darkness like they had in the Passover, and that's what you're seeing come right now], *but the Lord shall arise upon you [O Jerusalem], and His glory shall be seen on you."*

You know, in this dense darkness, when that glory comes on you, people will see a light on your face. When you walk by someone, the demons are going to get so upset that they are going to fall over. You'll just say, "Out in the name of Jesus," and keep walking. The glory is going to be that strong. And remember in John 17:21-22—when the two become one (Jew and Gentile), the same glory that is on Jesus will be on you.

3. **By demonstrating the power of God through miracles.** This earns the right to share the Gospel with not just Jewish people but any people group. I can go into an auditorium filled with unsaved Jewish people and God will demonstrate miracles. Then I can share the Gospel for two hours and the majority will stand up and pray a prayer of salvation. Don't tell me Jewish people aren't open to the Gospel! Christians just have to be normal—normal as defined by the Bible. That's all God is asking us to do.

4. **By sharing a proper presentation of the Gospel,** which I will teach you in the next chapter. But you can't present the Gospel in 99.9 percent of the cases to a non-Christian or someone who hasn't been raised in the church unless you've earned the right through a demonstration of God's Kingdom with signs and wonders. This is why the supernatural is so important.

I want to end this section with a prayer. This is going to change some of you dramatically if you have ever been anti-Jewish. If you have ever said things against Israel and the Jewish people, in God's eyes that is a sin and I want to lead you in a prayer of repentance. Some of you will even get physically healed as you repent.

Repeat after me:

> *Dear God, I'm so sorry I ever said or did anything against the Jewish people or Israel. Please forgive me. I believe the blood of Jesus washes away my sins and breaks the curse from the sins of my ancestors. And now that I am free from the curse, Lord Jesus, fill me with more and more of Your Spirit and give me a Jewish heart. Give me the heart of Esther. In Yeshua's Name, amen.*

Your greatest miracle is an invitation to participate in God's great salvation plan for all humanity. Will you embrace this? I want to mentor you to operate in the supernatural so that you can be a part of God's end-time strategy to usher nations into the Kingdom of God. Don't let this overwhelm you; yes, it's a big assignment, but you are called to start wherever you are. Start in your business. Start in your home. Start in your neighborhood. Start among your friends and family. Start what? Start stepping out in the supernatural, but also start praying for a new perspective on Israel, the Jewish people, and God's end-time plan. He wants to pour out His Spirit in ways we've never seen before. Let me bring it closer to home for you: *He wants to pour out His Spirit on you in ways you have never imagined!*

Your greatest miracle is an invitation to participate in God's great salvation plan for all humanity.

It's time for us as a community of believers to start being normal. It's time for us to change the way we present the Gospel—we need to show, then tell. We need to demonstrate, then share.

For too long, the Gospel has been presented as words without power. God is changing things. We are stepping into a season where we don't have the luxury of more time. It seems like God's moving things quickly. Jesus told me, "I'm coming back soon." God needs you. We need you!

Notes

1. For an in-depth study of this phenomenon with many documented examples, see John McTernan, *As America Has Done to Israel* (New Kensington, PA: Whitaker House, 2008).

2. Unless otherwise noted, the following historical references are from Steffi Karen Rubin, *Anti-semitism* (San Rafael, CA: Jews for Jesus, 1977), 32-33.

3. John Chrysostom, qtd. in Malcom Hay, *Europe and the Jews* (Boston: Beacon Press, 1961), 27.

4. F.E. Talmage, ed., *Disputation and Dialogue: Readings in the Jewish-Christian Encounter* (New York: Ktav Publishing House, Inc., 1975), 18.

5. Martin Luther, qtd. in *Encyclopaedia Judaica,* vol. 8 (Jerusalem: Keter Publishing House Jerusalem Ltd., 1972), 693.

6. Adolph Hitler, *Mein Kampf,* translated by Ralph Manheim (Boston: Houghton Mifflin Co., 1971), 65.

Chapter 9

YOUR SUPERNATURAL HEART TRANSPLANT

In the previous chapter, I explained why it's important to share the Messiah with Jewish people. In this chapter, I'm going to teach you *how.* When you do this, it's going to open up a door of blessing in your own family so that many of them will come to know the Messiah. I promise you this—when you learn how to communicate the Messiah with Jewish people, you will know how to communicate the Messiah better with *all* people.

Getting Ready to Share the Gospel with My Orthodox Jewish Father

When I was a new Jewish believer in Messiah, I was involved in starting one of the first modern Messianic Jewish congregations in America. A group of us wanted a congregation for Jewish people where we could have what we were used to in the traditional synagogue. I was the leader at the time and I knew nothing. So we hired a wonderful Messianic Jewish rabbi who did something unusual. Week after week, he proved that Jesus was the Jewish Messiah and never used the New Testament. He always spoke from the Jewish Scriptures—the Old Covenant.

My wife was raised Southern Baptist. When she got to college, her atheistic professors talked her out of her faith. Just in case there was a God, she called herself an agnostic rather than an atheist. When we got married, I insisted that she convert to Orthodox Judaism. So you might say she was a Southern Baptist, agnostic, Orthodox Jew. But, kicking and screaming, she would go with me to our Messianic Jewish congregation where she heard for the first time why the Bible is from God. If it's not from God then there is no foundation in Judaism or Christianity or anything else. Then, that same Bible proves through a multitude of predictions (prophecies) that Jesus is the Messiah. She came to a point one day where she said, "I have no choice. I have to believe."

When I got saved, I was very outspoken in my faith. Coming from an Orthodox Jewish background, my father was horrified that I was a believer in the Messiah, Jesus, and that I was so public about it. But one day he said, "I want you to tell me why Jesus is the Messiah." I thought, *I've been waiting for this day for so long!* I had been praying that he would come to know the Messiah as my mother did. But Mom would try to protect me by saying, "Your dad will never become a believer in that Jesus." She just didn't want me to be disappointed.

I remember telling her, "You're wrong. Dad *will* receive Jesus." How could I be so sure? Because I had been saying it for so long that I began to believe it. There was no evidence to my natural eyes. Dad was an Orthodox Jew who was born in Poland and saw everything that Hitler had done. There was no way he was going to believe. But something in me said, "I know my father is going to be a believer in the Messiah."

 There is no explanation for the survival of Israel except that God is real.

Prophecies That Have Come True About Israel and the Messiah

So I got a Tenach—that's a copy of the Jewish Scriptures. The Tenach is the same as a Christian Old Testament except that the books are in slightly different order and the verses could be one ahead or one behind. I said, "Dad, did you know there are thousands of predictions about our Jewish people and they all have come true?"

He replied, "No, I didn't know that."

I said, "Let me show you a few of them. God said in Deuteronomy 28 we would be the most blessed people on the face of the earth if we would follow Moses and the Torah, but if not, we would lose our Temple (we did); we would lose our city, Jerusalem (we did); and we'd be scattered to the four corners of the earth (we were). Whatever country we would go to we would be persecuted (we were). You see how precise and specific this is? But there is more.

"God said, even in the midst of all this, He would guarantee a sign that would confound the world. He promised that as long as there is a sun, moon, and stars, there would be a physical Jew on the face of this earth. You would think that after 2,000 years of the world trying to kill us because we're Jews that every Jew in the world would have assimilated or died, and there'd be no physical Jews. There's no logical explanation that a Jew still survives except for God's promise.

"Then God said through His prophet in Isaiah 66:8, 'Shall a nation [Israel] be formed in one day, at once?' And then in Isaiah 11:12, God says He's going to present a miracle banner to the world to grab their attention. He says He *will set up a banner for the nations, and will assemble the outcasts of Israel, and gather together the dispersed of Judah from the four corners of the earth.* We have seen that fulfilled on May 14, 1948. Against impossible odds, Israel became a Jewish nation in one day and the Jews from the four corners of the earth were still kept, not assimilated, and were gathered to their homeland, Israel. That's our God!

"The moment our nation was established, we had to fight for our lives against impossible odds. We didn't have money, we didn't have ammunition, we barely had clothing. We came from Europe with the clothing on our back and we were outnumbered. Twenty Arab nations with a combined population of 140 million declared war on us. These nations were rich with petrodollars and armed to the teeth. There is no explanation for the survival of Israel except that God is real.

"And when we first returned, the land was desolate. American author Mark Twain described it as a 'God-forsaken barren wilderness.' But Isaiah 35:1 predicted that *the wilderness and the wasteland shall be glad for them, and the desert shall rejoice and blossom as the rose.* Did you know Israel can grow vegetation in the desert? How did Isaiah know about the agricultural miracles that Israel would accomplish? Speaking about the blossoming of the rose, did you know that Israel is a major exporter of cut flowers to the world? Look how precise God's Word is.

"Then He said the waste cities that were totally flattened were going to be restored. Have you seen Tel Aviv and Jerusalem? These are modern cities. God said He would bring back the captives of His people Israel, and they would build the waste cities and inhabit them—even the Jews from the north. You know what's directly north of Israel? Russia! The greatest exodus we've seen in modern times has been the Russian Jews coming back to Israel. And by the way, if you think these predictions were written after the fact, we have the Dead Sea Scrolls that prove otherwise. No one has tampered with them.

"These are predictions by God and they have come true precisely. And just as God had a plan for the Jewish people, He has a plan for the Messiah because He wants to restore us to the Adamic nature. You know what life Adam had before the fall? He wasn't afraid of anything. He wasn't ashamed of anything. God wants to return us to that."

> In this new covenant, God said He would put the Torah inside of us and we would know Him. Not just know about God, but know God.

The New Covenant

"At the first Passover, we Jewish people put blood on the doorpost because the blood atoned for (covered) our sins. And the Angel of Death passed over our homes when he saw the blood. If you had lived in Egypt and Moses said 'I want you to kill a lamb and I want you to put the blood on the doorpost' and you refused, your firstborn would have died. Without the shedding of blood there is no forgiveness of sin. The blood of the lamb is a shadow of Yeshua's blood."

I continued to ask my Orthodox Jewish father, "Did you know that the Torah says clearly that the animal sacrifices will not stop until the Messiah comes? In Daniel 9:26, it says the '*Messiah* [the Anointed One—that's what Mashiach means] *shall be cut off* [die], *but not for Himself* [very important]; *and the people of the prince who is to come shall destroy the city and the sanctuary.*' In AD 70, the prince, Titus, and his Roman legions did exactly what Daniel prophesied. Just before this, Jesus had become our once-for-all-time atonement for sin, inaugurating the new covenant foretold by Jeremiah 31:31-34. In this new covenant, God said He would put the Torah inside of us and we would know Him. Not just know about God, but know God. It's the most wonderful thing.

"Under this new covenant, because the Temple is destroyed, you either have to say your sins are not atoned for because without the shedding of the blood there is no forgiveness of sin (see Lev. 17:11), or you have to say Messiah has come. Those are your only two options. And God said, 'I will not just cover your sins under this new covenant; I, God, will remember your sins no more.' I like that! I might remember them, but God says, 'They don't exist in My realm. That's why I can live inside of you and I can come to know you.'

"The Jewish way of knowing God is found in Jeremiah 31:33, '*I will put my law in their minds, and write it on their hearts.*' In other words, the Word of God (Torah) will not be outside of us but *inside* us! When the Messiah lives inside of us, it is the same as the Torah living inside of us. Ezekiel 36:26 describes this supernatural heart transplant: '*And I will give you a new heart, and I will put a new spirit in you. I will take out your stony, stubborn heart and give you a tender, responsive heart'* (NLT).

"In other words, once you have the New Heart and New Spirit, you can respond to God. When we had our natural heart, God called it *'deceitful'* and *'desperately wicked'* (Jer. 17:9). We all need this supernatural heart transplant. We all need to have 'experiential knowledge' of God.

"How can you know for sure who the Messiah is? Good question. The ancient rabbis saw predictions that when the Messiah comes there will be peace on earth. They called him Messiah Ben David (Messiah, son of David). Then, they saw other predictions that said when Messiah comes He will be like Joseph. They called him Messiah Ben Joseph. Joseph was betrayed by his own Jewish brothers and was sold for a few pieces of silver. Then he was put in a pit and left for dead. But he rose to power to be the savior of the Jewish people. So the ancient rabbis concluded there must be two Messiahs. They were almost right. How about *one* Messiah with *two* appearances?

"Moses said because we Jewish people wouldn't follow him, God would raise up another leader from among the Jewish people who would be greater than Moses. Why greater? Because the Torah says we must follow this One because God's Word will be inside His human body. Deuteronomy 18:17–19 says, *'And the Lord said to me: "What they have spoken is good. I will raise up for them a Prophet like you* [like Moses] *from among their brethren, and will put My words in His mouth, and He shall speak to them all that I command Him. And it shall be that whoever will not hear My words, which He speaks in My name, I will require it of him."'*

"There are over 300 specific prophecies of the Messiah in the Jewish Scriptures that were fulfilled by Jesus! According to Peter W. Stoner and Robert C. Newman in a book called *Science Speaks*, the odds of one man fulfilling only eight of the major prophecies about the Messiah are 1 in 100,000,000,000,000,000.[1] Jesus fulfilled 27 Messianic prophecies in a single day![2]

"God said the Messiah would be born in Bethlehem and gave a specific timeframe in the book of Daniel (Dan. 9:25). Did you know that there were several Bethlehems at the time Jesus was born? But the prophet Micah was so precise he said the Messiah would be born in Bethlehem Ephrathah of Judea (Mic. 5:2)!

"He would be despised and rejected by men (Isa. 53:3); live a sinless life (Isa. 53:9); be betrayed for 30 pieces of silver (Zech. 11:12-13); die by crucifixion (Ps. 22:16); have His clothing gambled for at the time of His death (Ps. 22:18). He would die before the Temple was destroyed (Dan. 9:26); arise from the dead (Ps. 16:10); and the majority of the Jews would not recognize Him (Isa. 53:3), but the Gentiles would follow Him (Isa. 11:10). All these things happened."

I continued, "Dad it's so important that you believe in Yeshua as your Messiah. Why? Because Daniel the twelfth chapter says those who are buried in the dust, some shall rise to everlasting life and some to everlasting condemnation. Everlasting is a pretty long time. So we all must choose."

My father grumbled and grunted a lot as I was speaking. At the end of our talk, he just walked away. But he was thinking about what I said.

We're coming into a time when the presence of God is going to be dripping upon every one of us and is going to jump off of us onto other people.

My Dad Has a Supernatural Heart Transplant

Many years later I got a call from my sister, Shirley. Our father was in the hospital in intensive care and he was dying.

Seven days before the phone call (I had no idea my dad was about to die), the presence of God just dripped all over me like I had only felt one other time in my life—when I first became a believer in the Messiah. But it was different this time. This presence was on me 24/7; it was almost like clothing I was wearing. For seven days I was walking around with this glory manifestation of God all around me. Then I got the phone call.

Shirley and I went to the hospital to have a few last words with Dad. His throat was so eaten up with cancer that he couldn't speak. My sister said, "Dad, Mom is in heaven. I'm going to be in heaven. Sid is going to be in heaven. Mom always said heaven must be such a wonderful place. We want you in heaven."

My father had no voice, but the presence of God that was on me dripped on him. I said, "Dad, do you want to make Yeshua your Messiah and Lord?"

And he said, "Yes."

I turned to my sister and said, "Shirley, he said yes!"

Shirley was a schoolteacher, and she's a stickler for details and so she responded, "I didn't hear him."

"Shirley, he's dying. This is good for Dad. Leave him alone!"

Shirley responded, "I did not hear him." Turning to our dad, she asked him, "Dad, do you believe Jesus died for your sins and is your Messiah and lives inside of you?"

He had no voice due to his disease, and yet he belted out a loud, "Yes!"

And then, my dignified sister started screeching at the top of her lungs, jumping up and down yelling, "Thank you Jesus! Thank you Jesus!"

I said, "Shirley, calm down. What are you doing?"

Then Shirley said, "I told God that when Dad receives the Messiah I'm going to jump for joy."

We're coming into a time when the presence of God is going to be dripping upon every one of us and is going to jump off of us onto other people. God wants you and me to be involved in the great unfolding of His redemptive story on earth. A key part of this story coming to pass is a church that operates in signs and wonders—not occasionally, but continually.

Remember, the Bible says that we Jewish people require a sign. Most Christians who are praying for signs and wonders don't know the true purpose for the miracles. God wants to use the supernatural to reach Jewish people so Jews and Gentiles can be united in one God—the God of Abraham, Isaac, and Jacob—and one Messiah, the Jew, Jesus.

What to Say, What Not to Say

As I explained in the previous chapter, there are 2,000 years of tragic history between the Church and the Jewish people. Most Jewish people are not rejecting Jesus, they are rejecting those who claimed to represent Him. It's going to take the presence of God to change things, and that's why I want to equip you in the supernatural. I want you to be able to do everything my *It's Supernatural!* television guests do—and do it better!

First, it's important to pay attention to the words that you use. Let me give you some tips on how to talk to a Jewish person.

Wisdom dictates you do not use the word *Christ* when trying to share the Good News with a Jewish person. Why? Because we have been called "Christ Killers" for 2,000 years. The word *Christ* comes from the Greek, but the word *Messiah* comes from the Hebrew. I *always* say Messiah and not Christ.

The name *Jesus* is not as offensive to Jewish ears as the word *Christ*, but it can still be a stumbling block. I like to refer to Jesus by His Hebrew name, Yeshua, when I talk to Jewish people. Because most Jews are not familiar with the name Yeshua, I usually start out with the name Jesus and then I introduce His Hebrew name.

There are other words that remind us of the persecution we Jewish people have endured over the centuries. For example, the word *convert* has a negative connotation because of being forced to convert or die. Instead, you can use the word *repent* or the phrase *turn to the Messiah*. Even the word *Christian* can be a stumbling block to some Jewish people. They may think you are asking them to stop being Jewish. A good substitute for "Christian" would be "believer in the Messiah."

Trinity is another offensive word. Even non-religious Jews know that Jewish people believe in only one God. The word *trinity* sounds to them like it is referring to three Gods. Instead of *trinity*, I use the phrase *triune nature of God*—one God who reveals Himself as Father, Son, and Holy Spirit. There are several Old Testament Scriptures referring to this triune nature. For example, Isaiah 42:1 talks about God (the Father) placing His Spirit on His Servant (the Messiah): *"Behold my Servant, Whom I uphold, My elect in Whom My soul delights! I have put My Spirit upon Him; He will bring forth justice and right and reveal truth to the nations"* (AMPC).

When you are sharing with a Jewish person, it is completely appropriate to refer to passages from the Tenach (Jewish Scriptures), which is virtually the same as the Old Testament in the Christian

Bible. Only in one place is there a serious incorrect translation in the Tenach. In the Christian Bible, Isaiah 7:14 reads, *"Therefore the Lord Himself will give you a sign: Behold, the virgin shall conceive and bear a Son, and shall call His name Immanuel."* As believers, we recognize this Scripture as a prophecy concerning the virgin birth of Jesus.

The same verse in the Jewish Bible—translated after the time of Jesus—says "young woman" instead of virgin. This removes the supernatural element of the virgin birth. How did the rabbis translate this verse before the time of Jesus? The Septuagint, the best Greek translation of its day completed by Jewish scholars before Jesus came to earth, uses the Greek word that is exclusively translated "virgin."

Jewelry to Start Conversations with Jewish People

I intentionally wear jewelry that will cause a Jewish person to ask questions. From there I can direct the conversation to the subject of Jesus. I do not wear crosses as jewelry. It is too objectionable to Jewish people because they have been accused of killing Jesus. Instead, when I wear jewelry I wear a Jewish star or menorah (seven-branched lampstand from the Temple).

There is power in testifying to what God has done.

Some feel the six-pointed Jewish star is pagan. But people say the same about the five-pointed star. And I don't hear anyone arguing that we need to remove the stars from the American flag! Actually, just because pagans have used thousands of symbols does not mean we cannot use them in a godly way. When you, as a Gentile, wear a Jewish star or menorah, a Jewish person might ask if you are Jewish. Your answer: "I have come to love the greatest Jew who ever lived!" That begs the question, "Who is the greatest Jew who ever lived?" What a perfect opening to talk about Jesus!

Now let me share with you the types of things I would say to Jewish people to lead them to Messiah.

My Supernatural Visitation from God

Wherever I go, I lead Jewish people to Jesus. And it is getting easier and easier! I typically start by asking if they have pain in their body. If they do, I pray and the pain usually leaves. Then I have an open door to share the Gospel.

You can also describe a miracle you have had in your life or that you have personally observed. And I encourage you to share your testimony, even if you are not Jewish. There is power in testifying to what God has done (see Rev. 12:11).

I often share my supernatural story of how I came to the Lord. I have been a Jewish believer in Jesus for more than 40 years. I became a believer after I had a visitation from God that turned my world upside down. On the worst night of my life I went to bed so fearful, I didn't want to live. I can't even express in words how hopeless I felt. My brief, desperate prayer was, "Jesus help!"

When I awoke the next morning, everything was different. My bedroom was flooded with the tangible presence of God. Every cell of my body was invigorated with His life. In this atmosphere of God's love, fear could not coexist. This was life-changing. I instantly knew that Jesus was the Messiah and I wanted to know more of Him.[3]

If you want to see miracles you can share with Jewish people or learn how to demonstrate them yourself, I invite you to watch our television show, *It's Supernatural!*, on most Christian TV networks or on our website at www.SidRoth.org. Or download our free app for iOS and Android devices to watch our *It's Supernatural! TV Network* (ISN) 24/7 on your smartphone or tablet.

> There is a way to intimacy with God, and a way to fill that God-shaped hole. God desires that intimacy even more than you do.

Jew or Gentile, All Can Have Intimacy with God!

Just as God told us the history of the Jewish people and how to recognize the Messiah thousands of years in advance, He told us how to experience the presence, love, and friendship of God for ourselves.

God's original intent was to have an intimate relationship with man, and in the beginning Adam and Eve had this kind of relationship with Him. But when they disobeyed God, the beautiful intimacy they had with Him was lost. The subsequent history of humanity has been cursed. When people have not been preoccupied with the pain of hunger, natural disasters, disease, crime, and war, they have searched for comfort through worldly success, money, power, love, drugs, sex, gambling, and a host of other things that always leave people feeling more lost and empty than before.

There is a God-shaped hole in our hearts that only God Himself can fill. We are designed to know God. It is literally in our DNA. There is a way to intimacy with God, and a way to fill that God-shaped hole. God desires that intimacy even more than you do.

The Jewish prophets have told us how to be restored to our rightful relationship with God—we must get free of the sin in our lives. We are told our sins separate us from the holiness of God.

We all sin, but when God forgives you, you are reconciled with Him and you gain the power to be free. Only God can forgive and give you the power to be free. I have met many who have been set free from all kinds of sins, addictions, compulsions, and illnesses through the supernatural power of God. Now is the time to examine your life and remove any sin that separates you from experiencing the love of God. But you need supernatural help to be set free.

God's Remedy for Sin

- In the Old Covenant, only the blood of an unblemished lamb sacrificed in the Temple could *cover* our sins and provide reconciliation with God (see Lev. 17:11).

- Because the Temple was destroyed in AD 70, a New Covenant was needed.[4]

- God predicted this New Covenant through the Jewish prophets (see Jer. 31:31–34).

- In the New Covenant, the earlier animal blood sacrifice is shown to be a shadow or foretelling of the blood of Messiah (see Heb. 10:1–14). Jesus is called the *Lamb of God,* and He is the sinless Passover Lamb who God provided to die in our place and pay the penalty for our sins, which is death. He is the *only way* to receive salvation and forgiveness of sins.

The New Covenant that was predicted in the Jewish Scriptures would do three things the Old Covenant could not do. This is why it would be called "better" (see Jer. 31:31–34).

- First, God said He (His Word) would live inside of us. That's exactly what Moses predicted about the One who would be greater than him.

- Second, we would personally know Him. The Hebrew word for "know" is the same that is used when the Scripture says that Adam knew Eve and had intimacy with her.

- And third, He would so wipe out our sins that He would remember them no more! This is much better than only covering our sins as we did in the Temple sacrifices. And because the animal sacrifices that atoned for our sins had to be in the Temple, which was destroyed, the New Covenant is our *only* hope!

True Repentance

It's very important to understand the word *repentance.* Most Jewish people and most Christians do not. Repentance means to turn away from your sins. Someone may say, "I'm a pretty good person." You know what? Compared to someone else, maybe you are. You can always find someone who's worse than you. But compared to the righteousness of God, you're not a good person. That's why the Torah says, "There is none righteous, no not one."

Many would argue, "I don't do bad things." Let's look at the Ten Commandments. Have you ever lied? Even what's known as a little fib or white lie? Of course you have. Of course I have. It's a two-edged sword pointing to me and to you. Have you ever stolen anything? Of course you've stolen. Have you ever had sex outside of marriage? Have you ever participated in homosexuality? Have you ever dabbled in the New Age, fortune-telling, witchcraft, or pornography? Have you had addictions to drugs or alcohol? Repentance is to say, "God, You're right. I have committed sin and I turn, I repent from the sin." True biblical repentance is to not just turn from the sin and then next week turn back to the sin. That's not repentance. That's religion at its stinkiest.

Biblical repentance is to say, "Oh God, I have sinned against Your holiness and I am so sorry. I turn..." but then you keep turning, and you turn to God. Full repentance is to turn to God for the power not only to have your sin forgiven but to overcome the sin. We often don't turn far enough.

God says, "I want you to know Me." The Greek word for "know" means experiential knowledge. John 17:3 in the Wuest translation reads, *And this is eternal life, namely, that they might be having an experiential knowledge of you."* Most believers have head knowledge of Jesus. But God wants you to have experiential knowledge of Him.

We must know God. If you do not know God before you die, I promise you, you will not know God after you die. There is a book called the Book of Life. Is your name in this book? Because those who are buried in the dust, some shall rise to everlasting life and some to everlasting condemnation (see Dan. 12).

> To be forgiven and reconciled with God is to experience His love, peace, and friendship. This is how to really live for the first time in your life.

Yes, there is a heaven where God is. But what makes you think you're going to be where God is? He says "Be ye holy for I am holy." Holiness has nothing to do with the length of your hair or whether you have tattoos. Holiness has to do with following the Ten Commandments, and you can't do it by yourself. You can only do it by repenting. Turn away from the sin and turn toward God for the power to overcome.

The choice for you is everlasting life or everlasting condemnation. Knowing about God or knowing God. Walking in fear or having God inside of you. Walking in unbelief or having the presence of God with you 24/7.

How You Can Be Right with God

The penalty for sin is death, permanent separation from God, and it can *only* be removed by acting in accordance with God's instructions in which an unblemished lamb dies in our place. We must exercise faith in God's provision through the New Covenant. The unblemished Lamb of God who died in your place is the Messiah, Jesus.

To be forgiven and reconciled with God is to experience His love, peace, and friendship. This is how to really live for the first time in your life. Are you ready to be forgiven and reconciled to God?

I have personally experienced the promise you are about to read from the Bible in my own life. I know this will also be true for you. How do I know this? God loves you as much as He loves me.

The Bible promises in Romans 10:9,13, *"If you confess with your mouth the Lord Jesus and believe in your heart that God has raised Him from the dead, you will be saved. ...'Whoever calls on the name of the Lord shall be saved.'"*

God has taken the first step. Now it is your turn. You may or may not feel anything. The feelings and experiences will come as you grow in knowing God by reading the Bible. Your first step is based on a decision.

> *Today I have given you the choice between life and death,*
> *between blessings and curses. ...You can make this choice*
> *by loving the Lord your God, obeying him, and commit-*
> *ting yourself firmly to him. This is the key to your life*
> (Deuteronomy 30:19-20 NLT).

Tell God you are sorry for your sins and ask Him to forgive you. He will! The blood of Jesus will wash you clean, and God will no longer see your past sin. Now say this prayer out loud and enter into the joy of the Lord.

> *Gracious God, I am a sinner. Please forgive me for my sins. I believe Jesus died for me and by His blood I am forgiven. You remember my sins no more. I ask You, Jesus, to live inside of me. Give me a new heart. Take over my life. I make You Lord of my life. Amen.*

Welcome into the *Mishpochah* (family) of God!

Are you ready to find out God's end-time book to the Church?

Hint: it's not the book of Revelation.

Keep reading!

Notes

1. "What are the odds surrounding Jesus Christ? Who was this child *really?*", December 6, 2016. www.christiananswers.net /q-aiia/jesus-odds.html.

2. For a list of the 27 prophecies, visit www.TheyThoughtForThemselves.com/27.

3. To read more about my supernatural encounter with Messiah Jesus and for a more extensive presentation of the Scriptures proving the Bible is from God and Jesus is the Messiah, go to www.TheyThoughtForThemselves.com.

4. The animal sacrifice of the Old Covenant had to be in the Temple in Jerusalem, and in AD 70 both the Temple and the city were destroyed. Interestingly, according to Daniel, the Anointed or the Messiah had to come and be cut off (die) before the Temple and Jerusalem were destroyed: *"Messiah shall be cut off, but not for Himself; and the people of the prince who is to come* [Titus and his Roman legions in AD 70] *shall destroy the city [Jerusalem] and the sanctuary [Temple]"* (Dan. 9:26).

Chapter 10

YOUR ESTHER ANOINTING

For if you remain completely silent at this time, relief and deliverance will arise for the Jews from another place, but you and your father's house will perish. Yet who knows whether you have come to the kingdom for such a time as this?

—ESTHER 4:14

I know this is going to surprise many of you, but *the* end-time book to the Church is...the Book of Esther. When I teach about Esther, I see more healings than when I speak on the subject of healing. And the message of this Old Testament book is very timely and significant for where we are in history.

Get ready. This last chapter is not intended to simply give you information. It's an invitation for you to take your place *for such a time as this.* The hour you're living in is the very purpose for which you were brought to the Kingdom.

The Hidden Mysteries of Esther

During the holiday of Purim each year, we Jewish people read the Book of Esther. Most of you will recall the compelling story in which Esther, a Jewish orphan, became queen of ancient Persia (modern-day Iran). God uniquely placed Esther in position to intercede on behalf of the Jewish people when they were threatened with extinction.

Jewish people normally have two names—a Hebrew name and a name from the country we have immigrated to. For example, my Hebrew name is Israel and my American name is Sidney. Esther's Hebrew name was Hadassah, which means "a myrtle with a beautiful fragrance." But her Persian name was Esther, which came from Ishtar, the fertility goddess. Today, we use the English version of "Ishtar," or "Easter," for Resurrection Day. That fertility goddess is why we have Easter bunnies and Easter eggs. In effect, you could say that Esther was dressed in a pagan cloak. No one knew she was Jewish; her heritage was hidden.

The hour you're living in is the very purpose for which you were brought to the Kingdom.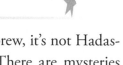

When the name Esther is translated into Hebrew, it's not Hadassah. Instead, it's a word that means "hidden." There are mysteries hidden in the Book of Esther.

I believe that **Esther is a magnificent type of the Gentile Church**. Why do I say that? First, no one knew about her connection to the Jewish people. Over the centuries, the Church has hidden its Jewish connection.

Second, **Esther was beautiful**. And whether you know it or not, in God's sight you are beautiful. Esther was a virgin. Though your sins be as scarlet, Church, they shall be as white as snow. Church, you may have been the biggest sinner in town, but once you accepted what the Messiah of Israel did for you, God says, according to the Jewish prophet Jeremiah, "I, God, remember your sins no more." They're not just covered like they were through the Temple sacrifices in the Old Covenant. God says we are now under a better covenant with better promises. God wipes away our sins so that they no longer exist.

Esther had a call, an assignment from Almighty God. She was the only one who could go to the king on behalf of the Jewish people.

Esther walked in divine favor. And you, Church, walk in divine favor. Esther was an orphan, a "no people" who was grafted into royalty. Church, do you know a "no people" that was grafted into royalty as a son or daughter of the King of kings?

Esther had a key to hearing God's voice. Church, I want you to have that same supernatural key. Esther soaked in oil of myrrh and in perfume for a year. As she soaked, she began to smell more like Jesus than her old nature. That's why it's so important for you to listen to anointed music and "soak" or pray in tongues in God's presence. We studied this earlier on in this book.

That reminds me of the parable of the ten virgins. Five were wise and five were foolish. The wise had plenty of oil and were prepared when the bridegroom appeared. Why? They were soaking in the Spirit of God. They were worshiping God all the time. They were reading the Bible. And they were only saying things that were pure and lovely and of good report. By the way, the moment you pray in tongues you enter into God's presence!

Did you know the myrrh plant Esther soaked in is bitter on the outside, but when it's crushed it is sweet on the inside? So Esther/Church, you may have been crushed for a while. But guess what? Tears may last for an evening, but joy comes in the morning (see Ps. 30:5).

In Esther 1:8, the guests at the king's banquet were told, "You can drink as much as you want." Church, you can be as filled with the Spirit as you desire. It's not just for special people. It's for those who hunger and thirst for a special God. There is no limit to how far you can go in Him.

And just like Esther was uniquely prepared to intercede for the Jewish people, Church, you are called to evangelize the Jew. There has never been a better time!

> The Jewish person God Himself has had cross your path is not an accident. He wants you to love them to Jesus.

Spiritual Scales Are Coming Off

Most believers do not realize we are at the fullness of the Gentiles (see Rom. 11:25). For years, I have conducted "Lectures on the Supernatural" all over the world. I rent a hotel auditorium and advertise the lecture to Jewish people. I promise that many who attend will be physically healed. Usually, 20 to 200 unsaved Jews are instantly healed. When this happens, I introduce them to the Healer—Jesus—and present the Gospel. Then 70 to 99 percent stand up and make public professions of faith. We usually have from 20 to over 1,000 unsaved Jewish people at our events. Sadly, most have never heard the Gospel. After they make professions of faith, I usually give them a copy of my Jewish evangelistic book, *They Thought for Themselves*. This book will answer most of their questions. Then we offer to enroll them in a discipleship class and have a local congregation invite them to attend services. The past two and a half years from our outreaches, almost *seven thousand* Jewish people have made professions of faith. The restoration of the Tabernacle (family) of David to Messiah Jesus from Amos 9 has begun!

But the most rewarding Jewish evangelism is one on one. Recently, I flew to New York City. My taxi driver was a Russian Jew. He mocked me when I told him I believe in miracles. Then I asked him if he had pain in his body. He told me his shoulder had been hurting for eight months. As he drove to the airport, I touched his shoulder and asked him to test it. He yelled, "It's a miracle! No pain!" He quickly said a prayer of salvation with me.

Then on the plane ride home, I sat next to a German Jew. At the start of the conversation, he was claiming that the Scriptures have been tampered with and are not from God. But before we landed, he said a prayer of salvation and said, "I hope someday I will have ten percent of the faith you have." I told him about my evangelistic website, TheyThoughtForThemselves.com, and he promised to read my book of Jewish testimonies online.

Thank God for the Esther anointing! Thank God this is His time to reach Jewish people. The Jewish person God Himself has had cross your path is not an accident. He wants you to love them to Jesus.

The Gifts and Calling Are Irrevocable

Many people give money to organizations providing humanitarian aid for Jewish people in Israel, and rightfully so. Many pray for Jews to return to Israel. Many have participated in "bless Israel" meetings, and we need that. Others have prayer meetings for Israel, and those are wonderful. But Suzette Hattingh, who used to be the lead intercessor for Reinhard Bonnke's ministry, once said, "Prayer without evangelism is like an arrow shot nowhere." If you have seen the supernatural blessings for blessing natural Israel, watch what happens when you give to evangelize the Jew!

Most people don't know this but there is a God-given call for every Gentile believer in Jesus that is found in Romans 11:11—salvation has come to the Gentile to provoke the Jew to jealousy. So the job of the Gentile believer is to provoke the Jew to jealousy.

The job of the Jewish believer is found in John 4:22: *"Salvation is of the Jews."* The Jew is called to reach the Gentile. Now many people think, "Perhaps the Jews lost their calling because so many rejected the Messiah." Romans 11:29 says the opposite: *"The gifts and calling of God* [it's talking about the Jewish people here] *are irrevocable."*

And by the way, if the Jews do their job and reach the Gentiles, and the Gentile Christians do their job and reach the Jews, guess what? We reach the whole world. God, You're so brilliant!

There is an anointing on Jewish people, whether they are aware of it or not, because the gifts and calling of God are without repentance (see Rom. 11:29 KJV). Look at the high percentage of Jews who have won Nobel Prizes and the technology coming out of Israel. The computer industry is booming in Israel. Some of the greatest inventions the world has ever seen are coming from Israel. So if their fall is riches for the world and their failure riches for the Gentiles (because Gentiles were grafted in), how much more their fullness? How much greater blessing when they receive their Messiah? It will be life from the dead. You're going to see the dead come back to life! You're going to see the same miracles Jesus did and even greater.

Revival broke out among the Gentiles when the Jewish people were spared.

God's Supernatural Door to Revival and Outpouring: "To the Jew First"

In the Book of Esther, the king sealed an order with his ring that all the Jewish people would be killed. Once he sealed that law, it could not be changed. But there was a higher law. In Esther 9:5 it says that the Jews were equipped with the sword so they were able to defend themselves.

The sword is a type of the Word of God. And when you equip Jewish people with the Word of God, the Law of Evangelism comes into play. What is the Law of Evangelism? Romans 1:16 says, *"I am not ashamed of the gospel...for it is the power of God to salvation... for the Jew first."* When you go *to the Jew first* it opens a supernatural door to revival among the Gentiles. This is what happened in ancient Persia. Esther 8:17 says, *"Then many of the people of the land became Jews."* Remember, the only way to know God back then was to be Jewish. Revival broke out among the Gentiles when the Jewish people were spared.

Amos 9 talks about the restoration of the Tabernacle of David. The word for "tabernacle" in Hebrew means "house" or "family." Who is the family of David? The Jewish people. God says, at the fullness of the Gentiles, the spiritual scales will come off the eyes of Jewish people. When enough Jews are saved, it leads to Amos 9:13:

"'The time will come,' says the Lord, 'when the grain and grapes will grow faster than they can be harvested'" (NLT). It's never been like that before. Gentiles will be standing in line to be saved when the Jewish people become who they were created to be.

The word *Jew* comes from the Hebrew word *Yehuda*, which means "a worshiper of God." Why is anti-Semitism so strong in the world right now? Because the devil knows his worst nightmare is when we Jewish people walk into our destiny. He's trying to kill every Jew that he can. I recently read that the Baltics are rewriting history, proclaiming that Adolf Hitler was a great man. The headline in a Ukrainian newspaper quoted a pro-Russian general saying, "Ukraine Run by Miserable Jews." In England, a headline said, "We're Leaving Britain. Jews Aren't Safe Here." Anti-Semitism in Europe right now is worse than it was just before Hitler took over. Israeli Prime Minister Benjamin Netanyahu said, "The only safe place for a European Jew is Israel." It is interesting to note the setting of the Book of Esther is Persia—modern-day Iran. Iran has publicly stated they want to destroy Israel. The Jewish people desperately need to defend themselves with the sword of the Spirit. *Esther, what are you waiting for?*

> Why is anti-Semitism so strong in the world right now? Because the devil knows his worst nightmare is when we Jewish people walk into our destiny.

Overcoming the Enemy to Your Esther Anointing

Esther, it's time to step out in the anointing and power God has already provided! What prevents believers from flowing in this anointing? A dangerous end-time deception that, I believe, is the enemy to the Esther anointing being unlocked and released.

You might think it's the devil; surprisingly, it's not. Certainly, the devil is behind this mass deception that is gaining increasing popularity among Gentile believers in Jesus. Simply put, I believe that one of the greatest enemies to your destiny being fulfilled and God's assignment being completed on Earth is *not* understanding the "signs of the times" you are living in. Let me explain.

Earlier in the book, I mentioned the sons of Issachar from Israel's history. They were recognized as those who *"understood the signs of the times and knew the best course for Israel to take"* (1 Chron. 12:32 NLT).

Could it be that your understanding of the end times plays a key role in whether or not you fulfill God's ultimate assignment for your life and, ultimately, His assignment for the nations? Is it possible that false or incorrect eschatology (study of the end times) could keep you from actually fulfilling the call of God and seeing the release of miracles we long to see?

Once again, this is not a side issue or a minor detail.

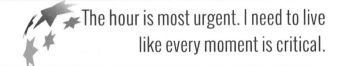

The hour is most urgent. I need to live like every moment is critical.

Avoiding End-Time Deception

Your end-time theology will be wrong if you do not distinguish between the Jew, the Gentile, and the Body of Messiah. This is where replacement theology teachers miss it *big!* Anyone who believes God has *replaced* Israel and the Jew with the Church will miss *all* the end-time action. At the first coming of Jesus, everything took place in Israel and the Jew was front and center. At His return, *all* the action again will take place in Israel and the Jew will be front and center. Just read the eleventh chapter of Romans and it *replaces* replacement theology!

What you believe about the end times will impact your involvement in God's activity on earth. Believers are literally missing out on their opportunity to flow in signs, wonders, and miracles, not because God is unwilling to release this power, but because they have incorrect views about the end times that create apathy. The hour is most urgent. Personally, I don't know when the Lord is returning. All I know is what I believe He has spoken to me. Three times, in a very vivid dream, the Lord said, *"I am coming back soon."* I cannot tell you what God's "soon" is, but I figure if He said "soon," I need to live like every moment is critical.

> The fullness of the Gentiles is here. Now, it's time for us to step out and take our place as those called to the Kingdom for such a time as this.

The Jewish Express

A friend of mine heard a report from a man who was a child during the Holocaust in Germany. Every Sunday morning as they were singing in church, a train would pass by and they would hear wailing and moaning. The trains were loaded with Jews headed for the death camps. And you know what the pastor said? "Sing a little louder" so they wouldn't have to hear the cries.

I've seen another train—the Jewish Express. It's loaded with Jewish people with *L'Chaim* (life), with the life of God within them. The tracks are being laid out right now. The tracks are going all over the world as Gentiles get mature in the Messiah, as Esther stands up. Esther 4:14 says that we are headed into the Church's greatest hour: *"For if you remain completely silent at this time, relief and deliverance will arise for the Jews from another place, but you and your father's house will perish. Yet who knows whether you have come to the kingdom for such a time as this?"*

I believe there is a unique *Esther anointing* upon every believer in these last days—this includes you! It's available to *whoever* will take his or her place in God's unfolding end-time plan. It's an anointing that will be accompanied by great demonstrations of power, favor, and miracles. When believers collectively operate in this Esther anointing, we will see the revival we've all been yearning for. It's not waiting on God; it's waiting on us. The fullness of the Gentiles is here. Now, it's time for us to step out and take our place as those called to the Kingdom for such a time as this.

Esther, I tell you the greatest move of God's Spirit is about ready to hit this earth. Are you going to be part of it? Stand up, Esther. Stand up for the Jewish people. Let God know that you have reached maturity.

As I am writing this book, a prophet friend of mine gave me a word. I believe this word is just as much for you:

Laban said to his son-in-law Jacob in Genesis 30:27: *"Please stay, if I have found favor in your eyes, for I have learned by experience that the Lord has blessed me for your sake."* What Laban was saying is still true. God promises in Genesis 12:3 to bless those who bless the Jewish people.

God will bless you because He has blessed Jacob. Remember, Jacob's new name was "Israel." I too and many of our partners have learned through experience that the Lord will bless you because you have blessed the Jewish people. You have done it with the greatest Jewish blessing by investing in Jewish evangelism, by partnering with me in ministry! God says in Proverbs 11:30, *"he who wins souls is wise."* Even more so at the fullness of the Gentile age, at the set time to favor Zion!

Let me paint you a picture of what is about to take place. We are entering into the times of miracles like we have never seen before. We are entering into the time of creative miracles! And I believe Jewish evangelism is the catalyst. *I believe Jewish evangelism is your catalyst to seeing the release of supernatural power and miracles that God desires!*

I see a time coming shortly when football stadiums will no longer be used for sporting events. They will be used to worship God. The tangible glory of God will be manifest in a physical way over these stadiums that will be seen for miles. The sick will walk in or be carried in and without human agency they will be instantly healed. People with emotional problems—some who have been hospitalized for years—will be instantly healed.

Our church buildings will not be large enough for all the new believers. Classrooms in colleges, high schools, and elementary schools will be invaded by the presence of God. The mushroom of the glory cloud will hang over entire cities. People will weep and repent and whole cities will come to Jesus.

My vision is big. But it doesn't catch God by surprise. Our God is *big!*

The Esther Anointing

And now I'm going to pray a supernatural prayer over you that I've prayed over many people and God has changed their hearts. It is called "The Esther Anointing." Are you ready to receive it?

I pray in Yeshua's Name that everyone who is reading this with an open heart right now will receive the Esther anointing. They will realize they've been called to the Kingdom for such a time as this. Father God, I pray You will give them Your heart, Your compassion for their Jewish neighbors, Jewish doctors, Jewish merchants, Jewish schoolmates, and Jewish business associates.

I pray that Jewish people will walk up to them and say, "I feel something wonderful radiating from you. What is that? Why do you love Jewish people so much?"

I pray in Yeshua's name that everyone who has ever said something anti-Jewish, anti-Semitic would repent right now. (Tell God you're sorry. Ask Jesus to forgive you.)

I pray Father God that everyone who receives this anointing will take part in filling up the Jewish Express. Jewish people are going to be won to the Lord and they will be like modern-day "Paul the apostles" who will go to the four corners of the earth and do a quick work. In Jesus' Name I pray. Amen!

ABOUT SID ROTH

Sid Roth has been on the cutting edge of Jewish evangelism for over 40 years. Most recognizably, he is the visionary behind and host of the internationally syndicated TV program, *It's Supernatural!*, which currently airs over 180 times per week worldwide. Sid is also a *New York Times* best-selling author and founder of the 24/7 *It's Supernatural!* Television Network. Sid's driving passion is see souls eternally transformed by the Messiah and believes the key to worldwide evangelism and the Lord's return involves going "*to the Jew first*" (Rom. 1:16 KJV).

For more about Sid and to view archives of his TV program, *It's Supernatural!*, please visit SidRoth.org.

Watch Our 24/7 TV Network
Wherever You Go!

Download our *It's Supernatural! Network* (ISN) App for iOS and Android devices!

ISN streams over 700 archived episodes of *It's Supernatural!* as well as new original worship and soaking programs, supernatural teaching courses, mentoring sessions and more.

Through the ISN App, you can:
- Stream ISN in HD.
- Watch episodes of *It's Supernatural!* TV on demand.
- Listen to *Messianic Vision* radio broadcasts.
- Stay connected to Sid Roth through social media.

Search "Sid Roth" in your device's App store and download the *It's Supernatural! Network* (ISN) App today!

You can also watch on your computer at **SidRoth.org/ISN.**

Watch Our 24/7 TV Network Wherever You Go!

Download our *It's Supernatural! Network* (ISN) App for iOS and Android devices!

ISN streams over 700 archived episodes of *It's Supernatural!* as well as new original worship and soaking programs, supernatural teaching courses, mentoring sessions and more.

Through the ISN App, you can:
- Stream ISN in HD.
- Watch episodes of *It's Supernatural!* TV on demand.
- Listen to *Messianic Vision* radio broadcasts.
- Stay connected to Sid Roth through social media.

Search "Sid Roth" in your device's App store and download the *It's Supernatural! Network* (ISN) App today!

You can also watch on your computer at **SidRoth.org/ISN**.

ABOUT SID ROTH

Sid Roth has been on the cutting edge of Jewish evangelism for over 40 years. Most recognizably, he is the visionary behind and host of the internationally syndicated TV program, *It's Supernatural!*, which currently airs over 180 times per week worldwide. Sid is also a *New York Times* best-selling author and founder of the 24/7 *It's Supernatural!* Television Network. Sid's driving passion is see souls eternally transformed by the Messiah and believes the key to worldwide evangelism and the Lord's return involves going "*to the Jew first*" (Rom. 1:16 KJV).

For more about Sid and to view archives of his TV program, *It's Supernatural!*, please visit SidRoth.org.